# Solving the American Health Care Crisis

**Also by Umang Malhotra**

Individual, Society, and the World

# Solving the American Health Care Crisis

*Umang Malhotra*

iUniverse, Inc.
New York   Bloomington

iUniverse books may be ordered through booksellers or by contacting:

iUniverse
1663 Liberty Drive
Bloomington, IN 47403
www.iuniverse.com
1-800-Authors (1-800-288-4677)

ISBN: 978-1-4401-8018-7 (sc)
ISBN: 978-1-4401-8019-4 (hc)
ISBN: 978-1-4401-8020-0 (ebook)

Printed in the United States of America

iUniverse rev. date: 10/28/09

# Acknowledgment

Many thanks to the hundreds of friends and acquaintances–amongst them doctors, nurses, lawyers, drug company executives, media people, and many other people of common sense–with whom I had sometimes heated discussions about topics related to health care, over a period of 4 years. My sincere thanks to several editors, especially Lesley Christiana, who carefully edited the entire manuscript while making constructive suggestions. Finally, I am thankful to my nephew, Dhruv Malhotra, who assisted me with any computer glitches that occurred while I was writing the book.

*Solving the American Health Care Crisis* is dedicated to the people of the United States, who deserve the best health care system in the world.

# Solving the American Health Care Crisis

# Contents

Preface.............................................................................. xi

Chapter I.　Introduction...............................................13

Chapter II.　Multinational Comparisons of Health Care
Systems...............................................................17

Chapter III.　Health Care Systems in Different Countries.....28

　　　　　Australia ..............................................................28
　　　　　Canada..................................................................33
　　　　　Cuba.....................................................................38
　　　　　England..................................................................40
　　　　　France ...................................................................48
　　　　　Germany ...............................................................53
　　　　　India......................................................................58
　　　　　Japan.....................................................................63
　　　　　Norway .................................................................70
　　　　　Spain.....................................................................77
　　　　　Sweden .................................................................81
　　　　　Conclusions about the health care systems in the
　　　　　countries considered ..............................................87

Chapter IV.　The American Health Care System ....................88

　　　　　General information................................................88
　　　　　Other statistics.......................................................89
　　　　　Health care system .................................................89
　　　　　A little history .......................................................92
　　　　　Medicare, Medicaid, the VHA, and SCHIP...............94
　　　　　Doctors, hospitals and clinics................................106
　　　　　Faith-based and private institutions ........................107

Challenges ................................................................107

**Chapter V.**   **Problems and Issues Related to the American Health Care System ...........................................108**

The effect of rising health care costs........................112
Bureaucracy and paperwork.....................................116
Fragmentation and eligibility inefficiencies in
entitlement programs .................................................119
Fraud and abuse in entitlement programs................122
Prescription drugs PART D for seniors and the
disabled .....................................................................124
Advertising and drug companies ..............................129
Lobbyists and their influence on officials and
legislators...................................................................136
Health insurance industry and insurance policies ....139
Bankruptcies..............................................................143
Doctors, lawyers, and malpractice lawsuits ............144
Other problems, issues, and mistakes made in the
delivery of health care ..............................................148
The role and use of information technology.............150
Myths and misconceptions .......................................151
The cost of competition.............................................156

**Chapter VI.**   **Different Approaches to Health Care Reform.159**

Secretary George Shultz's approach to health care
reform ........................................................................159
Senator McCain's Health System Reform ...............160
Critical comments on the Shultz-Shoven and
McCain Reform Proposals ........................................163
Massachusetts Health Care Reform Plan .................164
Key questions about the Massachusetts Plan and
its deficiencies...........................................................165
California's universal health care bill SB 840 .........167
Critical comments on California's universal health
care bill .....................................................................170
The Schwarzenegger-Nuñez Plan for California .....171
Flaws in the Schwarzenegger-Nuñez Health Care
Plan ...........................................................................173

Senator Tom Daschle's health care proposals ..........173
Critical comments about Daschle's health care
proposals...............................................................................176
Senator Clinton's Universal Health Care Choices
plan .....................................................................................177
Senator Barack Obama's plan ......................................180
Some discussion on, and solutions for, the Clinton
and Obama plans ..............................................................183
Closing comments on the health care plans
discussed above....................................................................185

**Chapter VII.  Cost Effective Solutions to the American Health
Care System ........................................................188**

**Recommendations ...............................................188**
Prevention and regular physical examination
reduce the cost of health care (especially for
people over forty years of age)....................................193
OECD guidelines for action ......................................197
Evolving concepts of universal health care in the
United States ..................................................................200

**Additional recommendations ...........................203**
American infant mortality is a disgrace for a rich
country—but the solution is there..............................203
Role of information technology (IT) and
outsourcing...............................................................204
Web-based, cost effective, medical solutions...........204
Medical tourism can assist in cost cutting ................206
Biotech in emerging countries can help to cut costs 215
Alternative Medicine ...............................................216

**Issues necessary to cut the cost of health care and
make it efficient ...............................................217**
Fragmented federal and state entitlement programs 217
Politicians and lobbyists .............................................218
Health insurance industry and insurance policies ....218
Cost of prescription drugs and their hyped
advertisement ...........................................................219

Cost of malpractice lawsuits and insurance.............221

**Chapter VIII. Conclusions**..........................................**223**

Some questions to ask in the search for a solution...224
Action needed ..............................................225
The task ahead................................................226
Closing comment............................................227

**Epilogue** .......................................................**231**
**Reference Notes**..........................................**237**

# Preface

When people ask me where I am from I say, "This world is mine." I lived much of my life in the rich countries of Sweden, Norway, and England; I also spent time in other European countries and traveled extensively in Western Europe, and other parts of the world.

I stayed nearly fifteen months in the United States from 1978 to 1980, and visited regularly after that. During that time, I met many doctors socially, from all fields of medicine. Often the conversations turned to health care, vitamins and supplements, and medications that people were taking in America. We never talked about health care in Scandinavian countries! These discussions intrigued me. What bothered me most was the drug companies' aggressive advertising of drugs; I never noticed hyped drug advertisements in Western European countries.

In Europe during the 80s, I fought against discrimination. I filed a case against the Norwegian State, which resulted in Ex-Prime Minister Odvar Nordli and Ex-Foreign Minister Thorvald Stoltenberg appearing as witnesses in the court of Norway. I also had a case against the Royal Bank of Scotland (RBS) that ended up in the World Intellectual Property Organization (WIPO) in Geneva. RBS lost the case 3–0 with the WIPO panelists. These were personal cases, but I hope that the outcomes benefited others too. In my book, *Individual, Society, and the World*, I said that my own motto became, "Think globally,—Act locally, in a humane and practical way."

Frank Rosenow was my best friend. He had traveled all over the world, and we sailed together for nearly twenty years. It was a shock to me when he died of a brain tumor at a relatively early age, in late 1993. He developed severe headaches while in Seattle, Washington, and he did not have American health insurance. His diagnosis took ten days, and it was too late for treatment by the time they put him in a wheel chair, on a flight home to Sweden. To an extent, I think this is one thing led me to write this book. I wondered at the time, how the health care system in America could be so inept that it could not treat my friend, irrespective of his insurance.

For more than nine years, I have been living in beautiful San Diego, California, where I often walk down the Dr. Martin Luther King Jr. Promenade. Inscribed on stones along the way are many of Dr. King's wise statements. One of the inscriptions says, "An individual has not started living until he can rise above the narrow confines of his individualistic concerns to the broader concern of all humanity." Apart from my own desire to write about the American health care System, Dr. King's words inspired me to present a common sense book, which points out the major problems and issues pertaining to the American health care system. The book is an objective analysis, from an outsider, who is interested in presenting cost effective and efficient solutions to the American health care crisis that cover every resident in America.

# Chapter I

# Introduction

*"Health care is a right and not a privilege."*
*Senator John Kerry speaking at a Democratic Party Unity Dinner*
*on March 25, 2004.*

During one of the presidential debates between President Bush and Senator Kerry in October 2004, Bush said that "Ours is the best health care system in the world," in response to a question from the moderator. Kerry did not challenge Bush's statement. Politicians often play on the emotions and patriotism of the people. Had Kerry challenged Bush's statement and reminded the audience that the statement did not make sense according to facts about the American health care system, he would have lost votes. No country's population likes to hear that their system is not good enough, especially when their leading politicians state it.

The United States of America is the richest country in the world, with one of the highest GDPs per person. It has some of the brightest and best minds in the world. It has some of the finest medical schools, institutions, and hospitals in the world. America is one of the least bureaucratic countries, yet it spends over 16% of its gross domestic product (GDP) on health related expenditures. This figure is expected to rise to nearly 20% of the GDP of the United States within a decade. In 2005, it was projected that the federal government would be responsible for more than 50% of all spending in health related fields within the following five to six years. At the same time, more than 47 million people in the United States have no health insurance and millions more are underinsured. On average, the Western European countries, as well as Japan, and Australia, spend 8 to 11% of their GDP on health care. Despite these facts, people in other rich industrialized countries have an average life span that is two to three years longer than that of the people in the United States.

Besides the fact that the life expectancy rate of Americans is lower than Western Europeans and the Japanese, the infant mortality rate in the United States is nearly twice that of other rich countries. According to the *World Factbook 2008*, compiled by the Central Intelligence Agency (CIA), Cuba was one of forty-one countries that had a lower infant mortality rate than the United States that year. Singapore had the lowest infant mortality rate in the world, with 2.3 babies dying before the age of one for every thousand live births. Norway, Sweden, Iceland, and Japan, all had infant mortality rates that were less than half that of America, which was nearly seven out of every thousand babies dying before the age of one.

The 2005 World Health Organization (WHO) report on the world's health care systems ranked the United States number 1 in obesity and 35 overall. America scored low in other categories too, such as in fairness in health care, where it tied with Fiji at 54. This state of affairs in the American health care system is a black mark for American decision makers and politicians.

Former President Carter said, "America can learn something from Cuba's health care system." The press rarely reports such statements because most people would have to swallow their pride to accept that a poor, communist country like Cuba has a lower infant mortality rate than the United States, and that the average life span of a Cuban is the same as for an American.

T. R. Reid,[1] author of *The United States of Europe* writes in his book:

---

[1] *T.R. Reid has covered the U.S. Congress and four presidential campaigns for The Washington Post. He was head of the Post's London Bureau for several years. From 1990-1995, he was the paper's chief correspondent in Tokyo. He is also the author of three books in Japanese and five in English, including The Chip: How Two Americans Invented the Microchip and Launched a Revolution. He is now a popular commentator on National Public Radio and is the Post's Rocky Mountain Bureau Chief. He lives in Denver.*

> Sometimes Americans seem to be in a state of denial about what Europe has achieved. American presidents from both parties, for example, have repeatedly declared that the United States has "the greatest health-care system in the world." That claim is hard to support. The unified Europe has higher life expectancy, lower infant mortality, lower rates of heart disease and cancer, and health insurance that covers every person—all for about half as much per capita as the United States spends... Since the United States pays much more and gets much less in return, it might behoove American policymakers to stop bragging about their own health-care system long enough to take a look at what the EU nations have done.

Subsequent chapters of *Solving the American Health Care Crisis* present charts that show aspects of the health care systems in different countries. There is a brief presentation on how each of these systems work, especially those of the rich industrialized countries. The information presented brings up a couple of important questions: Why is the cost of health care per person so much lower in these countries than in America? What can U.S. policymakers learn from their foreign counterparts?

There is also an explanation of how the American health care system works, as well as why it has the highest cost per person in the world, followed by a discussion of the problems and issues relating to the cost of health. The latter are defined as:

- Aggressive drug ads on TV and radio, and in newspapers and magazines

- Lobbying and campaign contributions by drug and insurance companies

- The cost of malpractice insurance for doctors

- Frivolous lawsuits in courts

- Fragmented and complicated health care policies and entitlement programs

- Profits of insurance and drug companies

- Bureaucracy

- Lack of electronic health care records for patients

- The high cost of drugs

A look at all of these, as well as certain other problems and issues will reveal why the cost of health care is so high in the United States. Basic health care should not be based on any ideology or system—i.e. capitalist, socialist, or their branches—it is a basic need. All politicians and decision makers in the United States should be concerned with finding a cost effective and ideal solution to the health care problem. It requires urgent attention and resolution from decision makers, much more so than any other domestic issue in America.

In closing, suggestions and cost effective solutions to the American health care crisis are presented, ones that would benefit everyone in America. The solutions take into consideration the best practices of the health care systems of other affluent nations, and the implementation of information technology (IT), which has a key role to play in cutting costs and in making any health care system more efficient and cost effective.

Health care—like clean air and water, food and shelter, and education—is a basic need in any society, especially in rich countries that can afford it, and it is necessary for development into a more free and mature democratic society.

# Chapter II

# Multinational Comparisons of Health Care Systems

## (Expenditures and Outcomes)

International comparisons of health care systems offer important tools for decision makers and politicians for evaluating the performance of their own systems. The data on the following pages suggests in what aspects a country is doing well or poorly.

The Organization for Economic Cooperation and Development (OECD) brings together countries sharing the same principles of a market economy, pluralist democracy, and respect for human rights. It has forty members from industrialized countries, including the United States.

The data in figure 1 shows key aspects related to health care figures for many of the industrialized countries. Data about Cuba is also included because this country has done exceptionally well in caring for the health of its people even though it is an economically developing country ruled by the authoritarian government of Fidel Castro for more than four decades. Despite economic sanctions by the U.S. government, Cuba's infant mortality rate per thousand children is lower than that of the United States.

Sweden has one of the lowest infant mortality rates at 2.75 per thousand, and one of the highest life expectancies, 80.74 years. It spends 9.2% of its GDP on health care. In comparison, the U.S. has a much higher infant mortality rate of 6.30 per thousand, and one of the lowest life expectancy rates, at 78.14 years, while it spends 15.3% of its GDP on health care. The cost of health care in all nations is rising and in America, it is likely to reach nearly 20% of the GDP within a decade.

Figure 1

| Country | Life Expectancy | Infant Mortality* | Literacy Percentage | Health Spending** |
|---|---|---|---|---|
| Australia | 81.53 | 4.82 | 100 | 8.8 |
| Canada | 81.16 | 5.08 | 97 | 10.0 |
| Cuba | 77.27 | 5.93 | 97 | N/A |
| England | 78.85 | 4.93 | 99 | 8.4 |
| France | 80.87 | 3.36 | 99 | 11.1 |
| Germany | 79.10 | 4.03 | 99 | 10.6 |
| Japan | 81.04 | 2.80 | 99 | 8.2 |
| Norway | 79.81 | 3.61 | 100 | 8.7 |
| Spain | 79.92 | 4.26 | 97.9 | 8.4 |
| Sweden | 80.74 | 2.75 | 100 | 9.2 |
| USA | 78.14 | 6.30 | 97 | 15.3 |

Source: Health spending from *OECD Health Data 2008*, June 2008; other data
from the *World Factbook* (CIA) January 1, 2008
* per thousand live births
** as % of GDP / includes public and private

The previous chart does not specify life expectancy of males and females separately, showing only average life spans. Take note though, that the average for females is four to seven years higher than that for men in all of the countries mentioned. The CIA *World FactBook* clearly states this.

Figure 2

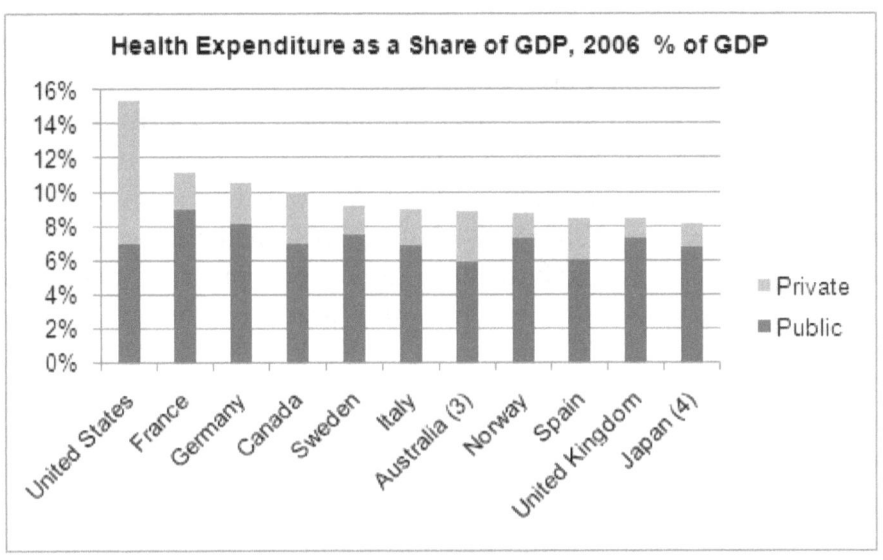

Source: Health spending from *OECD Health Data2008*, June 2008
(3) Data refer to 2005/06 (4) Data refer to 2005

Figure 2 gives the health care spending of most industrialized countries in that year. Spain's health care spending was 8.4% of its GDP, compared with 15.3% in the U.S., as of data sourced from the OECD.

The life expectancy and infant mortality rate for Spain were 79.52 years and 4.26 per thousand respectively, while health care spending was 8.4% of its GDP. In the case of America, the rates were 78.14 years and 6.30 per thousand respectively, while health care spending was 15.3% of its GDP. How is it that people in Spain live longer and have a much lower infant mortality rate than those in the United States, while spending half the amount per person on health care? It can't be only the eating habits of the American people.

In a study published by Dr. Michael Marmot and his colleagues in the *Journal of the American Medical Association (JAMA)* on May 3, 2006, they found that "Americans are much sicker than the English." This study covered large samples of white middle-aged males from England and America, and excluded less healthy Scotland and healthy Wales, which run their own parts of the National Health Service in Great Britain. In all diseases like diabetes, hypertension, heart diseases, myocardial infarction, stroke, lung disease, and cancer, Americans were reported to be much sicker than their counterparts in England were.

In another study by Harvard Medical School, researchers reported on May 30, 2006, in the *American Journal of Public Health* that Canadians are healthier than Americans are. This study reported that Americans are 42% more likely than Canadians are to have diabetes, 32% more likely to have high blood pressure, and 12% more likely to have arthritis. This study was based on a telephone survey of about 3,500 Canadians and 5,200 U.S. residents, eighteen or older, during 2002 and 2003.

The studies on English and Canadian comparisons of certain health parameters to those of America are the first of their kind done by researchers. Dr. Steffie Woolhandler, a co-author of the Canadian study, makes a point in stating that universal coverage makes it easier for more Canadians to get disease-preventing health services. One can draw the same conclusion about England, as there is universal health care coverage there too. Why are decision makers ignoring the facts on the state of the health care system in America?

Expenditure on health care is rising in almost all of the countries however; one of the biggest rises, in terms of percent, has been in the United States, where the percentage of people over the age of sixty is lower than in all the other industrialized countries mentioned in figure 1. Why then is the cost of health care rising much faster in the United States?

Figure 3 shows how costs have been rising for selected countries since 1960. Total expenditure on health care is shown as a percent of GDP (Includes private and public spending)

When compared to the sixties, health care expenditure in almost all of the countries increased by a factor of two to three times what it was in the beginning of that decade. Health care expenditure of most nations was stable from 1993 to 2000 except for in Australia, Germany, and Japan. These countries had special circumstances. In the case of Germany, it absorbed nearly 15 million people from Eastern Germany. Japan was in recession during most of the nineties.

Figure 3

| Country | 1960 | 1970 | 1980 | 1990 | 1993 | 2000 | 2002 |
|---------|------|------|------|------|------|------|------|
| Australia | 4.1 | N/A | 7.0 | 7.8 | 8.2 | 9.0 | N/A |
| Canada | 5.4 | 7.0 | 7.1 | 9.0 | 9.9 | 8.9 | 9.6 |
| England | 3.9 | 4.5 | 5.6 | 6.0 | 6.9 | 7.3 | 7.7 |
| France | 3.8 | 5.4 | 7.1 | 8.6 | 9.4 | 9.3 | 9.7 |
| Germany | N/A | 6.2 | 8.7 | 8.5 | 9.4 | 10.6 | 10.9 |
| Japan | 3.0 | 4.5 | 5.6 | 6.0 | 6.9 | 7.6 | 7.8 |
| Norway | 3.9 | 4.5 | 7.0 | 7.7 | 8.0 | 7.7 | 9.6 |
| Spain | 1.5 | 3.6 | 5.4 | 6.7 | 7.5 | 7.5 | 7.6 |
| Sweden | N/A | 6.9 | 9.1 | 8.4 | 8.6 | 8.4 | 9.2 |
| USA | 5.0 | 6.9 | 8.7 | 11.9 | 13.3 | 13.1 | 14.6 |

Source: Rising cost of health care from *OECD Health Data 2004*, 3rd edition

In the United States during the Presidency of Clinton (1993-2000), health care expenditure fell from 13.3 to 13.1 as a percentage of GDP. This was a period of unprecedented growth rates and falling unemployment.

The population of Australia, Canada, and the U.S. has grown by nearly 91.4%, 73%, and 59.4% respectively, since 1960. These countries have accepted the major portion of immigrants amongst OECD countries. Figure 4 shows population growth from 1960 to 2002.

Figure 4

| Country | Population in 1000's / 1960 | Population in 1000's / 2002 | Percentage increase |
|---------|---------|---------|---------|
| Australia | 10,275 | 19,663 | 91.4 |
| Canada | 18,180 | 31,414 | 73.0 |
| England | 52,449 | 59,232 | 12.9 |
| France | 45,684 | 59,486 | 30.0 |
| Germany | 55,433 | 82,489 | 48.9 |
| Japan | 94,302 | 127,400 | 35.1 |
| Norway | 3,581 | 4,538 | 26.7 |
| Spain | 30,455 | 41,874 | 35.5 |
| Sweden | 7,485 | 8,925 | 19.2 |
| USA | 180,674 | 288,369 | 59.6 |

Source: Population growth from 1960 to 2002 from *OECD Population Data 2003*

According to the table in figure 4, amongst the countries considered, England has the least increase in population from 1960 to 2002 at 12.9%, while Australia has the highest increase in population for that period, at 91.4%. Reports say that up until June of 2005, Australia admitted 120,000 immigrants as well as 14,000 refugees. As a percentage of Australia's population of just over 20 million, that is well above the share that America takes, which is approximately a million a year, but with a population fifteen times greater. The Australian economy has been booming for more than a decade, with average growth rates between 3–4% despite the intake of over a million immigrants in that period. The unemployment rate has been the lowest in almost thirty years. There has been no relationship between the intake of immigrants and growth in health care expenditure in Australia.

Immigration Minister Joe Volpe of Canada stated, "Immigration is a fundamental driver of the economy of tomorrow." Canada invited nearly 240,000 immigrants in 2005. This figure is approximately two and a half times that of the United States if one takes into consideration that the population of Canada was 32 million at the time, compared to 295 million for the United States. With an aging population and low birth rates, Canada has no choice but to take in a substantial number of immigrants.

Spain's population increased from nearly 30.5 million in 1960 to nearly 41 million in 2002, yet total expenditure in health care remained steady at around 7.5% of its GDP for a decade. In 2005, Spain granted amnesty to an estimated 800,000 immigrants working illegally. This was Spain's third amnesty in fifteen years. The Spanish economy has been performing well compared to other European Union (EU) countries for over a decade. Again, there has been no correlation between the intake of immigrants and expenditure on health care.

Germany and Japan have been the exceptions, where expenditure in health care increased substantially. The West German economy absorbed over 15 million East Germans after the fall of the Berlin Wall in 1990. The one to one conversion of the East German Mark into the Mark followed. In the case of Japan, the economy remained sluggish and in recession from 1990 to 2000, hence, the percentage rise in the cost of health care was higher than in other countries.

England had the least increase in population, with only 12.9% from nearly 52.5 million to 59.2 million, between 1960 and 2002. Health care expenditure increased at a higher percentage rate due to specific policies of the Labour government that came to power in 1996, but it was still much lower in the United Kingdom than the average expenditure of other rich countries of the EU.

The population of almost all the affluent countries of Europe, and of Japan and Canada, has stabilized. With their populations aging and with low birth rates, they either have started to decline, or will do so within the next five to ten years if not supplemented by immigration.

A study from the Center for Disease Control and Prevention (CDC) released in the first week of March 2006 concluded that foreign-born residents were healthier than native residents were. CDC Statistician Achintya Dey pointed out, "In general, immigrant adults in the U.S. are healthier than their U.S. born counterparts, but the longer they live in the U.S., the more their health resembles their U.S. born counterparts." Despite having less access to health care or insurance coverage, and generally being less well off, newly arrived immigrants have significantly better physical and mental health than the people born in the United States have. One could also say that even illegal immigrants are much less likely to burden the health care system, as they are much younger and possibly healthier, than the average person in the United States is. This point is made because some politicians have created the myth that immigrants— legal and illegal—largely contribute to higher health care costs by using emergency room health care services, while they ignore the fact that over 47 million Americans are uninsured and millions more under-insured.

It is clear that there is no correlation between increases in health care spending and the intake of immigrants (including illegal ones) into various countries. There is hardly any data from which to conclude that immigrants are to any extent responsible for the rising cost of health care. Most immigrants are younger than the average age in a particular country and are more likely to contribute to the growth of the economy than to be a burden on the health care system.

Figure 5

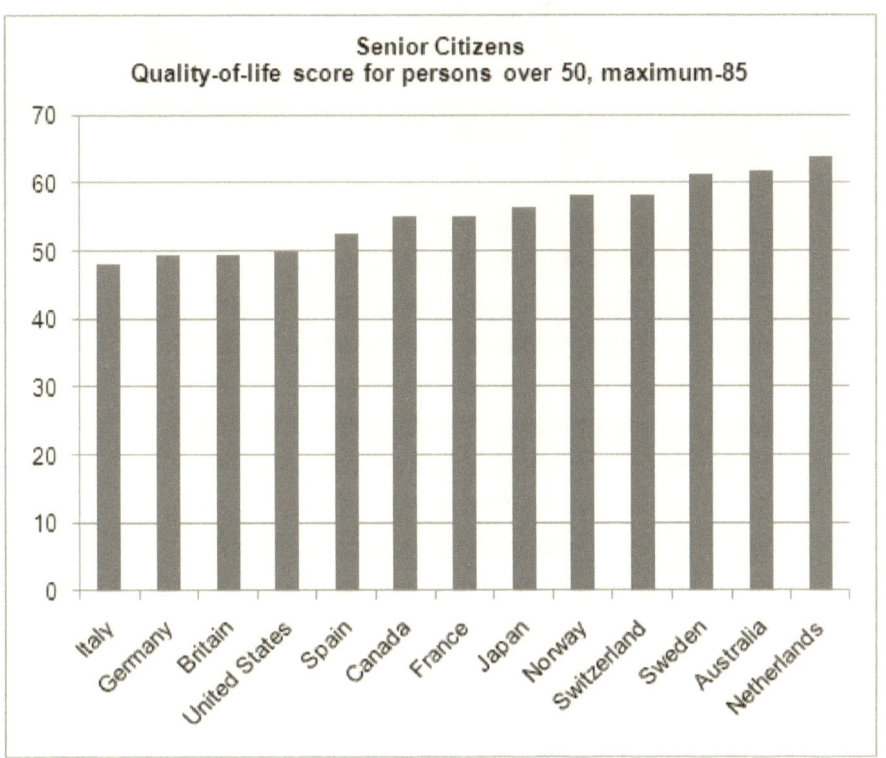

Source: AARP (2002)

Figure 5 charts the "Quality-of-life" score for people over fifty years old. It shows that the Netherlands looks after its older generation better than any other country, while Germany and the United States are among the four worst at providing for this segment of their population, according to a survey conducted by the AARP.[2]

It should be noted that America spent nearly 15% of its GDP in health related fields, yet it is nearly at the bottom of the chart when it comes to caring for its elderly. This means that the United

___

[2]     *The AARP was founded by Dr. Ethel Percy Andrus, a retired high school principal, in 1958. It evolved from the National Retired Teachers Association (NRTA) to the American Association of Retired Persons, later shortened to AARP, in 1999. Any body over fifty years old can be a member. The AARP has more than thirty five million members.*

States' return, as related to health care expenditure, is rather poor in relation to the other industrialized countries listed.

Figure 6

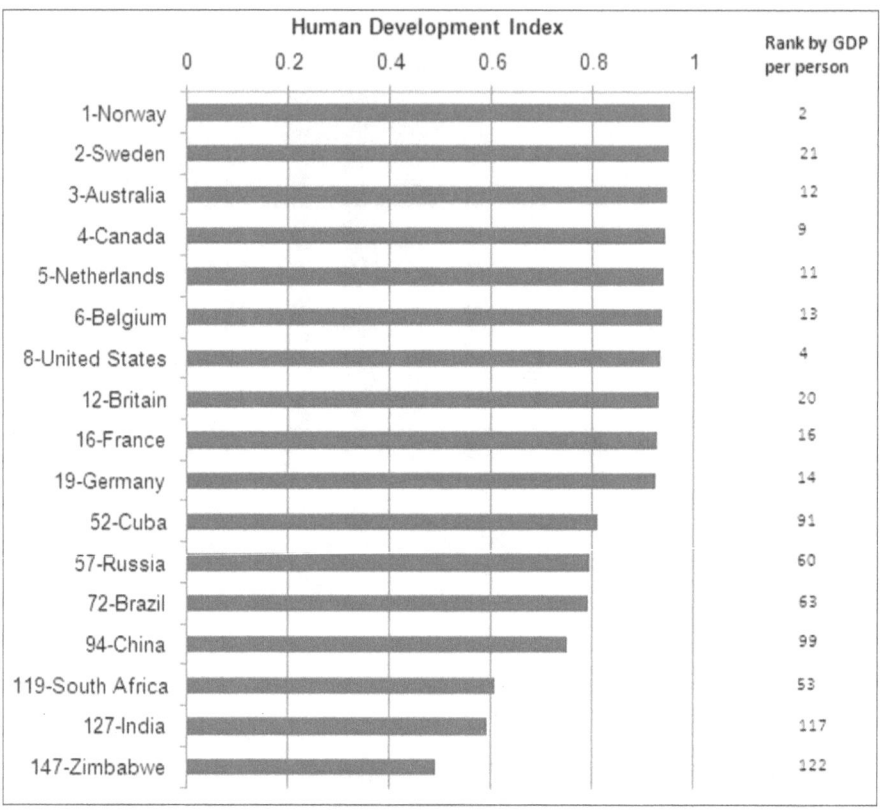

Source: Human Development Index (HDI) data from the United Nations Development Program (UNDP) 2002

The data in figure 6 is from the United Nations Development Program (UNDP). The Human Development Index (HDI) takes into consideration life expectancy and education as well as the GDP per person in a particular country. The chart shows that the United States is number eight in HDI, while Norway is number one. The variables chosen by UNDP for HDI are arbitrary. It could have also included variables like equal rights for women and minorities, elimination of poverty, environmental protection, and certain other parameters.

Health care of the population of any country should be, and must remain as, the key parameter in the evaluation of the Human Development Index. The quality of health care, both preventive and actual, is a basic need for longevity and the quality of life of the population. It is important for the decision makers of each country to evaluate and then implement the best possible solutions for their people. America can learn from the best practices and most efficient ways of delivering health care in each country, without regard to ideologies and dogmas. In short, America could combine the best practices in all aspects of health care, from any country, in order to develop a comprehensive and cost effective plan for all the people of the United States.

# Chapter III

# Health Care Systems in Different Countries

The following pages briefly present the health care systems of many of the rich industrialized nations and of Cuba and India, along with some vital statistics, background, and history.[3]

## Australia

For more than a decade, Australia had one of the fastest growing economies of the OECD countries, until 2008. The Australian health care system is regarded as being world-class, in terms of both its effectiveness and the efficient care of its patients. It is a mixture of public and private sector health services. The Australian government has the primary responsibility for developing broad national policies, regulation, and funding for the health care of its population.

### General information

Australia has a land area of 7,685,850 sq km, which is roughly the size of Western Europe or the U.S. (excluding Alaska). Tens of thousands of years ago, Indigenous Australians of aboriginal origin settled the country. People from Great Britain and subsequently other countries began settling in 1788, resulting in the present day population of over twenty million people.

### Other statistics

The population of Australia was 21,685,310 in July 2008, consisting of 92% Caucasians, 7% Asians, 1% Aboriginal and 'others.' Nearly 25% of the people were foreign born and another

---

[3]    *Population statistics quoted in this chapter are taken from The World Factbook, by the CIA, and various OECD reports, unless otherwise referenced*

25% were first generation natives, with a net 6.34 migrants per thousand of population.

This means that between June of 2004 and June of 2005, Australia admitted nearly 135,000 immigrants (including refugees). With low unemployment and control of its borders, the Australian government expects that the country can take 250,000 immigrants per year, by 2025.

The gross domestic product (GDP) per person was equivalent to $37,300 according to 2007 estimates, with an unemployment rate of less than 5%, and a literacy rate of nearly 100%. The average economic growth rate has been between 3% and 4% for the last fifteen years.

The median age of the population was 36.78 years. The infant mortality rate was 4.82 per thousand live births, and average life expectancy was 81.53 years in 2008. For males, this was 79.16 years while it was 84.02 years for females.

There were just 400,000 Indigenous Australians at that time. Their life expectancy was twenty-one years less, while the infant mortality rate was twice that of the general Australian population. They also faired badly economically, with an unemployment rate three times as high.

**Health care system**

*Health care spending accounted for 8.8% of Australia's GDP for 2006, 67% of which was public spending according to the OECD. This figure was adjusted for purchasing-power parity, including both public and private spending.*

In 1946, Australia amended its constitution to enable the federal government to provide health benefits and services without altering the powers of its six individual states and territories. The federal government has a leadership role for developing broad national policies on health care. The states and territories are mainly responsible for the delivery and management of public health care and for maintaining a direct relationship with most providers, including the regulation of health professionals.

The goal of Australian health care funding is to give universal access to care while allowing choices for individuals through substantial private sector involvement in delivery and financing. This way, every resident has access to health care in Australia.

The major part of national health care is called Medicare, which provides high quality care which is both affordable and accessible to all people in Australia, often provided free of charge at the point of delivery.

General taxation revenue largely finances national health care that includes a Medicare levy based on a person's taxable income. Federal funding for Medicare consists of:

- Subsidies for prescribed medicines (with a safety net for the chronically ill) and free or subsidized treatment by practitioners such as doctors, optometrists or dentists (specified services)

- Substantial grants to the six states and territory governments to contribute to the costs of providing access to public hospitals at no cost to the patients

- Specific purpose grants to state and territory governments and other bodies

In addition, state and territory governments supplement Medicare funding with their own revenues for funding public hospitals.

For health care, the main consultative body between the federal, state, and territory governments is the Australian Health Ministers' conference (AHMC). All major health care funding agreements are bilateral between federal and each of the state and territory governments, with broad parameters agreed multilaterally by the AHMC.

Special arrangements cover members of the armed forces and veterans however, they remain eligible for mainstream Medicare coverage. The federal government finances residential care for the aged through subsidies paid to service providers. Federal, state, and territory governments jointly fund community care services to the aged and the disabled.

Medicare covers all permanent residents in Australia. It also covers, to a varying degree, citizens of New Zealand, visitors, and temporary residents. Reciprocal health care agreements between Australia and Great Britain, Finland, Sweden, Ireland, Italy, Malta, Holland and some other European nations cover visitors from those countries.

All people eligible for Medicare are entitled to a choice of free accommodation with free medical, nursing, and other care as public patients in state and territory owned hospitals, designated non-government religious and charitable hospitals, or in private hospitals that have made arrangements with governments to care for public patients.

Private health insurance is an important component of financing health care in Australia. Insured people have added benefits such as choice of doctor, choice of hospital, and the choice of timing of procedure. Private insurance can also assist with meeting the cost of private services not generally covered by Medicare. These services include dental, optical, physiotherapy and podiatry services.

The federal government maintains the principle of community rating by regulating insurance organizations. Community rating ensures that health funds must charge everyone the same premium regardless of health status or claims history. This makes certain that private health insurance is open to a wide range of people in the community, including the aged and chronically ill. In short, nobody is priced out of private health insurance.

The cost incurred by patients receiving private doctors' services, some optometric services, and dental surgery, whether in or out of hospital, are generally reimbursed, either fully or in part, by means of Medicare benefits. Private patients are free to choose or change their doctor whether in or out of hospital (provided that in the case of in-hospital care the doctor has the right to practice in the relevant hospital).

The federal, state, and territory governments encourage people to take private health insurance as well. For example, the federal government introduced a 30% rebate on private health insurance in January 1999.

For billing arrangements, patients may claim Medicare benefits by:

- Paying the doctor's account and then claiming benefit from Medicare

- Arranging payment to the doctor by Medicare, and then paying the balance

Medicare offices accept claims either by mail or over the counter. Alternatively, doctors can send the account directly to Medicare, accepting the Medicare rebate as full payment for the service provided to the patient.

The Pharmaceutical Benefits Scheme (PBS) provides all Medicare eligible persons with access to effective and necessary prescription medicines at a reasonable and nominal cost. PBS provides subsidies for most drugs. Estimates put the amount of PBS subsidized prescriptions dispensed in Australia at around 75% . The federal government pays over 80% of the cost. Patient co-payments fund the remainder.

All eligible people fall into one of two categories that determine the amount the patient contributes and the amount of subsidy paid for each prescription. The categories are:

1. Special category people who receive certain pensions, benefits, or cards administered by the Departments of Family and Children's Services (FACS) or Veterans' Affairs (DVA), or who meet certain criteria for being disadvantaged

2. General category patients pay the cost of medicines for each prescription up to a maximum amount per item

Special category patients pay a smaller amount per item than general patients do, and the PBS pays the balance up to the listed price. Special patient prescriptions comprise 80% of the total Government expenditure on the PBS.

Health care in Australia faces similar challenges to those in other modern rich nations, however funding, and administration of the Australian system results in health care equal to the best in the world in terms of facilities, quality, and professional standards of care. The Australian health care system has little waiting time for surgeries.

# Canada

Evaluation of Canada's health care system has been constant since its inception four decades ago, with the system undergoing continuous reforms in response to changes in medicine and society. The fundamentals however, remain the same, universal health care coverage for all residents in Canada based on need rather than on the ability to pay.

The publicly funded health care system is an interlocking set of ten provincial and three territorial health insurance plans, known to Canadians as Medicare. This system provides access to universal, comprehensive coverage for medically necessary hospital and physician services.

## General information

Canada has a land area of 9,984,670 Sq km, which is somewhat larger than the U.S. It is land of vast distances and rich natural resources. Canada became self-governing from the United Kingdom in 1867, while retaining ties with the British Crown. The issue of reconciling Quebec's French-speaking population with the English-speaking majority moved to the backburner after the Quebec government's referendum on independence failed to pass in 1995. Canada's paramount political problem is meeting public demands for quality health care and education.

## Other statistics

The population of Canada was 33,212,696 in July 2007, of which about 19% was foreign-born. It consisted of 28% British Isle, 23% French origin, 15% other European, 2% Amerindian, 6%

Arabs, and 26% mixed background. There was a net 5.62 migrants per thousand of population in 2007.

The median age of the population was 40.10 years. The infant mortality rate was 4.75 per thousand. Average life expectancy was 81.1 years. For males, this was 78.65 years while it was 83.81 years for females.

The gross domestic product per person was equivalent to $38,600, and the unemployment rate was nearly 7% in 2006. Canada exports nearly 85% of its goods and services to the U.S., and led the G7 (a group of seven rich industrialized nations) in economic growth in 2002. It was again nearly at the top of the growth rate in 2003 according to the Canadian Department of Finance.

**Health care system**

*According to the Canadian Institute for Health, Canadian health care spending accounted for 10% of Canada's GDP for 2006. This figure was adjusted for purchasing-power parity. Total health care expenditure per capita was just over 3,900 Canadian dollars.*

The federal department responsible for the health care system of Canada is called Health Canada. On their website, they describe their history and mission as:

> The Canadian parliament passed the Canada Health Act (CHA) in 1984, which is the cornerstone of the Canadian health care system, affirming the federal government's commitment to a universal, accessible, comprehensive, portable, and publicly administered health insurance system. The CHA aims to ensure that all residents of Canada have access to necessary health care on a prepaid basis by establishing criteria and conditions for the provinces and territories to satisfy in order to qualify for their full share of the federal transfers for health care services. Health Canada is the federal department

responsible for helping the people of Canada to maintain and improve their health.

Canada's federal government, as well as it's ten provinces and three territories all play an important role in the health care system. Health Canada describes the federal government's responsibilities as:

- Setting and administering national principles for the health care system through the Canadian Health Act

- Assisting in the financing of provincial/territorial health-care services through fiscal transfers

- Delivering health-care services to specific groups like veterans, Inuits, and First Nations

- Providing other health-related functions such as public health and health protection programs, and health research

Canada's federal, provincial, and territorial governments collaborate on various health care policy and programming issues through an annual conference of Ministers of Health and Care Services. Regular meetings of the Deputy Ministers of Health and Care Services support this collaboration. In addition, four advisory committees comprised of senior officials discuss health care issues on an ongoing basis, and provide advice directly to deputy ministers. They are:

- The Advisory Committee on Governance and Accountability

- The Advisory Committee on Health Delivery and Human Resources

- The Advisory Committee on Information and Emerging Technologies

- The Advisory Committee on Population Health and Security

The administration and delivery of health care services is the primary responsibility of each province or territory, which is guided by the provisions of the Canada Health Act. The federal government reimburses provinces and territories in the form of fiscal transfers.

Health care services include insured primary health care (such as the services of physicians and other health professionals) and care in hospitals, which accounts for the majority of provincial and territorial health expenditures. The provinces and territories also provide some groups (decided by authorities of the state) with supplementary health benefits not covered by the Act, such as prescription drug coverage.

Health Canada ensures that health services are available and accessible to First Nations (the collective term for all self-governing peoples of aboriginal descent in Canada) and Inuit communities. The Medical Services Branch administers the non-insured Health Benefits (NIHB) on behalf of the Minister of Health and Care Services. The program pays for certain medical services and products covered neither by provincial or territorial health insurance plans or programs, nor by any third party.

In short, health services are free at the point of delivery for all Canadian residents. General taxation revenue based on a person's taxable income finances the national health care system.

Local and regional clinics in the provinces and territories provide every aspect of health care information to the residents of Canada. Ministry of Health and Care Services toll free health care lines are also available.

There is active promotion by federal and regional governments of the preventive side of health care. The federal, territorial, and provincial governments have set a national target to increase levels of physical activity by 10% by 2010. The Health Canada website stresses the following points:

- Physical Activity: This reduces stress, strengthens the heart and lungs, increases energy levels, helps you maintain and achieve a healthy body weight—and it improves your outlook on life.

- Healthy Living: The magazine Health Canada has several publications and information to help people make informed choices in the field of food and nutrition, alcohol and drug abuse, mental health, safety and injury, sexuality and smoking.

Federal, provincial, and territorial governments have embarked on a national consultation process with the public to define public health goals for Canada. The consultative process involves three components:

1. Public Education

2. Consulting

3. Deliberations

Details of this process are available at www.healthycanadians.ca/aboutinitiatives.html

Despite majority support amongst the Canadian population for the universal health care system, it has been reported by the Fraser Institute, a free-market group that "Canadians wait an average of thirty-eight weeks between a visit to the family doctor and orthopedic surgery and they wait nearly two months to start radiation treatments for cancer after referral by a doctor."

In a case brought by a Canadian citizen, Mr. Chaoulli, in Canada's Supreme Court, the Court struck down a Quebec law banning private medical insurance. The high court stopped short of striking the constitutionality of the country's health care system.

It is difficult to ascertain the decision of the court on the health care system in Canada. Mr. Chaoulli, who was born in France, has long called for Canada to adopt a two-tier public/private health care system similar to those in France, Germany, and Switzerland.

The evidence in the case had shown that there were widespread delays in treatment of patients in the universal health care system.

Paul Martin, Canadian Prime Minister at that time, responded to the decision of the Supreme Court by saying that his government was making progress on decreasing wait times. He went on to say,

"We are not going to have a two-tier health care system in this country. Nobody wants that. What we want to do is to strengthen the public health care system."

# Cuba

On a visit to Cuba in May 2002, former President Jimmy Carter stated in a speech to the Cuban people, "Cuba has a superb system of health care and education."

Cuba has been included because while it is not a rich industrialized country like the others covered in this book, it has an excellent health care system, despite being a single party dictatorship under Castro for over four decades. The Cuban health care system is universal and free. The Ministry of Public Health administers it.

## General information

Cuba has a land area of 110,860 Sq km, which is slightly smaller than Pennsylvania. Christopher Columbus discovered Cuba in 1492. Spain ruled this country for several centuries. The native Amerindian population declined as African slaves were imported to work on sugar and coffee plantations, Spanish, and other settler moved in from other countries. Cuba gained independence in 1902. Fidel Castro has ruled since 1959 and there has been a net migration of people from Cuba since then.

## Other statistics

The CIA estimated that the population of Cuba was 11,346,670 in July 2005. It consisted of 51% mulatto, 37% white, 11% black, and 1% Chinese. The average life expectancy of the Cuban people was 77.27 years, while the infant mortality rate was 5.93 per thousand. The median age was 36.80 years. The 2007 GDP per capita estimation was equivalent to $11,000 in purchasing power parity, and the literacy rate was just over 98.8% of the population.

## Health care system

The Cuban health care system is nearly fifty years old. It was a policy decision, made by the government, that education and health care should be free for all Cuban people. Cubans receive free medical care, regardless of a person's socioeconomic situation. The health care system assures the equity, accessibility, and universality that Cubans require. The health indicators of the Cuban people have outstripped those of poor or economically developing countries. It is close in parity with most of the rich countries in the world, concerning life expectancy and infant mortality rates.

The health care system is administered through decentralization and community participation, via national, provincial, municipal, and peoples' health councils. All regions of Cuba have doctors, whether provincial or city. The ratio of doctors to the population is 1 per every 200 Cubans, according to studies conducted by researchers at Tulane University in New Orleans. The ratio of doctors to people in the U.S. is one to more than 400.

The Cuban health care approach includes not only equity, but also priority of care for the vulnerable groups of society, like women, children, and the elderly. There is an emphasis on childhood vaccinations. Almost all children receive vaccinations for diseases such as polio, tuberculosis, and measles.

Training programs have produced a large number of physicians, nurses, technicians, and other health care professionals. At any particular point, more than 2,000 Cuban health professionals serve in 57 countries, according to a Cuban Health Ministry report.

According to the American Association for World Health, the U.S embargo of Cuba has dramatically harmed the health and nutrition of large numbers of ordinary Cuban citizens. Furthermore, it states that for several decades the U.S embargo has imposed significant financial burdens on the Cuban health care system. The fall of communist rule in the Soviet Union further weakened the Cuban economy, due to loss of trade with the Soviet bloc countries.

Despite these upheavals, Cuba's health care statistics are impressive considering its poor economic situation. In 1997, Cuba managed to rank second best among seventy-eight economically developing countries, using the Human Poverty Index. The Index blend is composed of literacy rates, life expectancy, access to health care and safe water, and the percentage of malnourished children. Maintaining this health care system has been an impressive feat considering the Cuban economy diminished by one third in the 1990's.

# England

England is part of Great Britain, along with Scotland and Wales. Together with Northern Ireland, they make up the United Kingdom (U.K.), a leading trading power, financial center, and the largest investor in the United States. With Germany, France, and Italy it forms the quartet of trillion-dollar economies in Western Europe and is the world's fifth or sixth largest economy (France and the U.K. trade positions). The U.K. is a leading member of the European Community (EU) but it is not a member of the Euro currency.

Established In 1948, the National Health Service (NHS) was the brainchild of Aneurin Bevan, the Welsh-born Minister of Health and Care Services. The aim was to provide free health care for all residents of the U.K. based on need, not on ability to pay at the point of delivery. Waiting lists remain for some surgeries despite the fulfillment of this aim.

## General information

The United Kingdom has a land area of 244, 820 Sq Km, which does not include administrative territories. The area of the U.K is slightly smaller than Oregon.

The U.K. was the dominant industrial and maritime power in the nineteenth century, and played a leading role in developing democratic institutions. At its peak, the British Empire ruled one-fourth of the world. The U.K. was a founding member of the United Nations (UN), the North Atlantic Treaty Organization (NATO), and the Commonwealth.

## Other statistics

The population of the U.K was 60,943,912 in 2005. This included nearly 1.6 million Muslims and nearly 1.5 million people from other Asian countries. The U.K is increasingly becoming a multi-cultural society, with several million immigrants from its former colonies. The percentage of the population living in Scotland, Wales, and Northern Ireland was 8.5%, 4.9%, 2.9% respectively. Net migration was 2.17 migrants per thousand of population in 2008. Experts expect the population to stabilize within the next ten years unless there is substantial immigration into the country.

The GDP per capita was equivalent to about $35,000 in 2007, and the unemployment rate was around 5.3%. The population below the poverty line was estimated at 17%. The literacy rate was 99% of those who completed five or more years of schooling. The average real growth rate has been 2.5% for the past five years.

The median age of the population was 39.90 years. The infant mortality rate was 4.93 per thousand. Average life expectancy was 78.85 years, for males it was 76.37 years, while it was 78.46 years for females.

## Health care system

*Health care accounted for 8.4% of the United Kingdom's GDP for 2006, and is expected to rise to 9.2%. This figure includes both public and private spending.*

England, Scotland, Wales, and Northern Ireland have their own way of administering its health care services, which are similar in their collective aim to provide health care for all their residents based on need, and not the ability to pay. A wide range of health professionals, support workers, and organizations make up the NHS.

## Policy and guidance

*The Department of Health* is responsible for setting overall health and social care policy in England. Taxes fund the NHS, which the Department of Health manages. This means it is accountable to the parliament. It sets aims and targets for the NHS, and monitors performance through its four directors of health and social care. The NHS aims to bring the highest level of physical and mental health care to all residents, within the resources available, by:

- Promoting health and preventing ill-health

- Diagnosing and treating injury and disease

- Caring for those with long term-term illness and disability, who require the services of the NHS

Over 99% of the population uses the NHS for their health care needs. A private health care sector offers extra insurance.

The Labour government under Prime Minister Tony Blair pumped money into the NHS, and its budget rose in real terms by over 7% a year from 1998 to 2004, but its real output rose only 3.7% a year according to reports. Waiting times have fallen though, and people no longer wait years for operations. By 2005 the NHS budget was around £70 billion (British pounds), or $122.5 billion.

The Blair government's boldest step was to complement the internal market with an external one. In the internal market, hospitals and health care service providers compete within the framework of the NHS, which also contracts work to independent firms. By the end of 2005, private providers performed around 4% of publicly financed elective treatment. The *Economist* of May 7, 2005, reported that "Blair has shaken up an inefficient state-controlled NHS by introducing both an internal market—hospitals get paid per patient they treat, instead of through a block budget—and by letting the NHS participate in the external market—the state pays private companies to operate on NHS patients."

**How the NHS works**

The NHS is evolving the way it works, to make sure that patients always come first. The following diagram shows the current structure of the NHS. Health services in Northern Ireland, Scotland,

and Wales, structured along similar lines to those in England, have the same basic objectives.

Figure 7

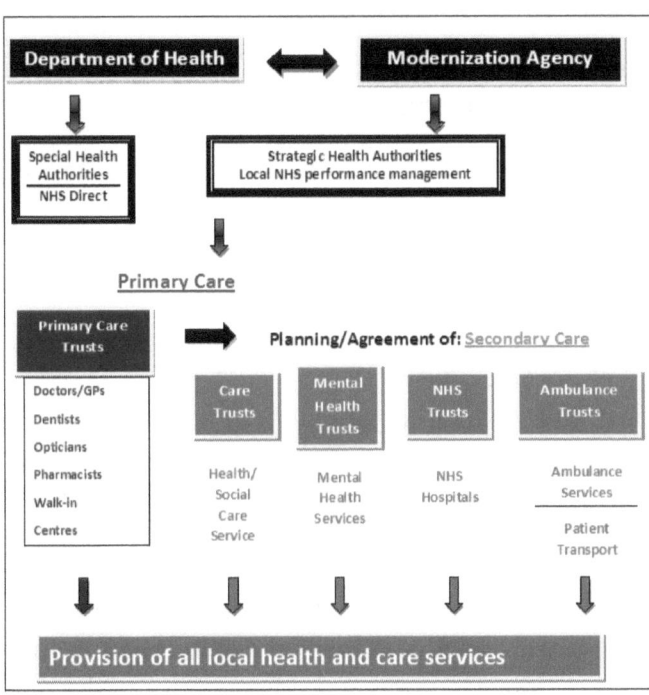

Source: flow chart from NHS website 2005

NHS facts and figures in a typical week are as follows:

- 1.4 million people will receive help in their home from the NHS

- More than 800,000 people will be treated in NHS hospital outpatient clinics

- 700,000 will visit a NHS dentist for a check up

- NHS district nurses will make more than 700,000 visits

- Over 10,000 babies will be delivered by the NHS

- NHS chiropodists will inspect over 150,000 pairs of feet

- NHS ambulances will make over 50,000 emergency journeys

- NHS district nurses will receive around 25,000 calls from people seeking medical advice

- Pharmacists will dispense approximately 8.5 million items on NHS prescriptions

- NHS surgeons will perform around 1,200 hip operations, 3,000 heart operations and 1,050 kidney operations

*Source: Above facts are from the Department of Health, as of April 6, 2004*

## How it works for patients

For primary care, the patient visits a local doctor, dentist, an optician for an eye test, or just makes a trip to a pharmacy to buy a non-prescription drug. The walk-in NHS Centers, and the phone line, NHS Direct, are also part of primary care. There is no cost for the patient to visit a doctor or a local doctors' surgery (operated by one or more doctors). After a check up, the doctor may give advice, prescribe medicine, or recommend the patient to a specialist for further examination. Doctors' surgeries are located in all parts of the country, within easy reach of people in every corner of England. There is also secondary care, with the recommendation of a primary care doctor, which includes elective and emergency procedures.

I gained firsthand knowledge of NHS care while living in England, on and off, over a period of four decades. The following are a couple of examples of what I experienced:

- After a car accident in England at the age of twenty-two there was glass in my right eye and cuts on my face. The doctor had to operate on the eye and put a dozen stitches beneath it. There are no scars on the upper part of my right cheek from the stitches, and my eye recovered completely, without any side effects. I stayed in the hospital for a week. My only complaint was that the quality of the hospital food was very poor, but then a lovely nurse brought me food from home!

- Years later, when I returned to England after spending time in Poland on business, I discovered that I had constant swelling in my jaws when I chewed or ate. Previous NHS medical check ups had shown no medical problems. I learned from my doctor that this happened because my glands had absorbed some poor quality water in Warsaw. He arranged an appointment for me with a specialist at Guys Hospital in London, who drained the fluid from my glands and gave me ultrasonic massage treatment. There has been no reoccurrence for over fifteen years.

I did not have to pay a single cent for the visit to the doctor in my neighborhood surgery, or for my stay or treatment in the hospitals. A garbage collector, professor, taxi driver, or a banker, or anybody else, gets the same treatment under the National Health Service in England, and it is completely free. A friend of mine holds a directors' position at a prominent hospital. I asked him whether he was going to have any supplemental health insurance, when the government introduced private top-up insurance over fifteen years ago. His answer was "What for?" and "Hell no!"

Every UK resident has the right to register with a local doctor, also known as a general practitioner (GP).

GPs look after the health of the people in their local community, and deal with a whole range of problems. They also give advice on every aspect of health care. GPs usually work with a team that includes nurses, health visitors, midwives, and other health professionals such as physiotherapists and occupational therapists.

Dentists treat patients' teeth and gums. There are both private and NHS dentists. With NHS dentists there are nominal charges for check ups, cleaning and work done on teeth and gums, however, all dental work is completely free if the patient is under eighteen years of age, a student, unemployed, poor or elderly, and a few other categories. Patients must pay a private dentist either from their own pocket, or through private insurance. Dentists can refer the patient to a see a hospital dentist, who does specialized work, such as surgery, straightening teeth, and more complicated bridge and root canal work.

Dental charges fall into three price bands, corresponding to the following three categories of treatment:

- A preventive package including check up, scale and polish, oral health advice

- Simple treatments such as fillings

- More complicated treatments such as bridges and dentures

Eye care—there are three types of eye care professionals. Optometrists carry out eye tests to check the quality of a patient's sight, look for signs of disease, which may need treatment from a doctor or eye surgeon, and prescribe and fit glasses and contact lenses. Dispensing opticians fit and sell glasses, and can give advice on the type of lenses, but do not test eyes or prescribe. If medical or surgical care for an eye disease or an eye injury is required, then a patient sees an ophthalmologist, who holds a Doctor of Medicine degree. There are standard charges for these services, unless the patient is prepared to pay from his or her own pocket for higher quality glasses and frames.

**Pharmacists and payment for prescribed drugs**

Pharmacists, also known as chemists, are experts in the field of medicinal compounds, and in how they work. They are responsible for filling the prescriptions given to people by their doctors. They play a key role in providing quality health care and ensuring the safe supply and use of medicines by patients. Pharmacists are in every locality, within a mile or two of almost every household, especially in urban areas. There are over 11,000 chemist shops in England and Wales. This works out to be one shop for each 5,000 people.

**Charges and exemptions**

GPs can prescribe any drug passed by the Medicines Control Agency, although it is up to the GP to decide whether its use would be of value. Drug prescriptions last for one month at time, and the GP can give the patient repeat prescriptions for up to six months before seeing the patient again. There is a standard prescription charge of £5.75, or about $10 per item. It does not matter how expensive the prescribed drug is. Everybody pays the same amount for each prescription item, whether a dustbin collector, or a company director.

People in the following categories are exempt from prescription charges:

- Children up to sixteen years old

- Students under nineteen in full time education

- People over sixty

- People on income support or family credit

- People getting jobseeker's allowance (unemployed)

- People receiving disability working allowance

- Pregnant women and women who have had a child in the past year

- War pensioners (for prescriptions related to their war disablement)

- Medical conditions including diabetes, epilepsy, permanent stomas, myasthenia gravis, Addison's disease, and thyroid conditions

Patients can also buy quarterly or annual prepayment cards for all prescription drugs at a reasonable price.

There are certain categories of patients exempted from fees when they go for dental or eye care. The Department of Health decides these categories, which are subject to change periodically.

**No fear for patients to see the doctor, dentist or eye care professional**

The residents of England have no fear in going to see their doctor at any time if they cannot afford to pay. The percent of the GDP per person has been steadily rising and aligns more now with the average GDP spending on health care of the other rich countries of Europe. The National Health Service is a sacrosanct English institution, despite the waiting time for certain operations. No politician can even talk about either dismantling the current health care system, or replacing it by a private system. Like the other rich European countries, England also faces challenges in controlling the rising costs of health care as the population ages.

# France

France was a leading member in creating the European Union (EU). French cooperation with Germany has proved central to the economic integration of Europe, which resulted in the introduction of a common exchange currency—the Euro. The French economy has enjoyed steady growth rates since World War II.

The French health care system has been in place for over a hundred years. It is constantly evolving, as are the health care systems in other rich industrialized countries. In June of 2000, the World Health Organization (WHO) classified it as "best health care system in the world." The general health of the French population is a testimony to its success, as the women have the second highest life expectancy rate in the world.

## General information

France has a land area of 547,030 Sq Km, which excludes areas of overseas administrative lands. The area of France is slightly less than twice the size of Colorado.

France embodied the "Declaration of the Rights of Man" on August 26, 1789, shortly after the storming of the Bastille prison, which began the French Revolution on July 14, 1789—otherwise known as Bastille Day. General Charles de Gaulle organized the resistance movement during the occupation of France by Germany during World War II. After victory in World War II with the help of the U.S., the Fourth Republic was established. In 1958, Charles de Gaulle initiated the Fifth Republic, which later led to the freeing of several of its colonies, including Algeria.

## Other statistics

The population of France was 60,656,178 in July 2005, of which nearly 10% were Muslim—mainly from Algeria and North Africa. There was a net migration of 1.44 migrants per thousand of the population. The French population is expected to stabilize within the next five to ten years, unless there is substantial immigration from other countries.

The gross domestic product per person was equivalent to $32,600 in 2007, while the unemployment rate was about 7.9%. It is the fifth to sixth largest economy in the world, and had a growth rate of nearly 2.1% in 2007. The population below the poverty line was 6.5% in the year 2000. The literacy rate was 99%.

The median age of the population was 39.2 years in 2007, and the infant mortality rate was 3.36 per thousand. The average life expectancy was 80.87 years. For males, this was 77.68 years, while it was 84.23 years for females.

## Health Care System

*Health care spending accounted for 11.1% of France's GDP for the year 2006. It was the largest percentage for health-care spending amongst the EU countries, apart from Germany.*

The French government is a guarantor for comprehensive health care rights for its population. It plays a crucial role in setting policies and provides overall supervision of the health care system. The Ministry of Health and Care Services exercises control over the relationships between funding institutions, health professionals, and patients. French residents have the right to choose between health care providers regardless of their income level. They can consult a variety of health care providers and can choose between public, private, university or general hospitals. It has also been reported that there is no waiting time to see a doctor, and that patients can make same day doctors' appointments. There is no waiting time for surgeries.

The parliament sets the target level of national expenditure on the health insurance system each year. On this basis, objectives are set for each specific activity, public and private hospitals, community medicine, pharmacy, and the health and social services network.

Health insurance is a branch of the French Social Security system. Funding for health care is done through proportional taxation on the salaries of the working population (60% of the fund), including retirement pensions and capital revenues, and by indirect taxes on alcohol and tobacco. More than 85% of the people have supplemental insurance, often provided by their employers, through private insurance companies. The poor and disadvantaged enjoy free universal health care, financed by taxes.

The government provides health insurance to three major population groups. These are:

- Salaried persons and their families

- Farmers, agricultural workers, and their families

- Artists, independent business owners, and their families

Within each of these three groups, expenditures are dispensed by region and type. They include general practitioners' fees, specialists' fees, medical prescriptions, public hospitals, private clinics, nursing professionals and medical transportation.

The state exercises its policy and funds through central, regional, and departmental services organized under the Ministry of Health and Care Services. Agreements that set the rules for health care distribution and the payment of fees govern relations between the health insurance system and health professionals. There are two organizations under the Ministry of Health and Care Services: General Health Management, and Hospital and Health Care Management. Under these organizations are numerous health care facilities and agencies that oversee and regulate all aspects of health care.

**Doctors or practitioners**

There were more 185,000 doctors at the beginning of the twenty-first century in France, or 3 doctors for every 1,000 inhabitants. This ratio is extremely favorable compared with that of the United Kingdom, the United States, Germany, and Italy.

Patients may choose their own medical practitioners. Those paying supplemental insurance have greater latitude in choosing their doctors, while others choose their practitioners operating within a 'fixed catchments' area. Doctors enjoy great freedom in the variety drugs that they can prescribe, but this principle is somewhat toned down by the body that regulates expenditure on prescription drugs. An organization under the Ministry of Health and Care Services fixes the reimbursable cost of drugs. The National Health Service sets the fees for different doctors. It is more expensive to see a specialist than a general practitioner. The Ministry of Health and Care Services reimburses only the standard fees, decided by the Ministry, to private doctors with their own fee schedules.

**Hospitals and clinics**

Three types of institutions deliver health care. These are public hospitals, private clinics and non-profit health care hospitals.

Regional, university, local and general hospitals fall under the category of public hospitals, which have evolved since the French Revolution. Funding for public hospitals comes primarily from health insurance funds.

A group of surgeons and obstetricians started private clinics, which eventually evolved into private hospitals. A 1991 law requires all doctors in private clinics to share medical files with their colleagues in public hospitals.

Non-profit hospitals were originally denominational. They make up nearly 15% of the inpatient services in the French health care system.

The extensive cooperation between the private and public sectors in the French health care system allows the population to avoid waiting lists for surgery. The private sector was responsible for treating more than 50% of surgeries and more than 60% of cancer cases in the year 2004.

Public sources predominately fund the health care system in France, but both the public and private sectors deliver the services.

## Top-up insurance and choice

Most residents of France also have supplemental, or top-up, insurance. This gives them more choice in all kinds of health care services. The premiums for such an insurance policy depend on age and the level of coverage required. An important principle of supplemental insurance is that the state pays its share for any health care services and the insurance companies pay the difference.

For the patient, the French health care system is extremely beneficial. The French public gives high marks to their system, as compared to the public of other countries in the EU and in America.

Despite hospitals waiting lists being almost non-existent, and doctors still making home visits, the French health care system is facing financial crisis. The state reimburses about 75% of general medical costs, 100% of the costs for the poor; supplemental insurance policies cover the rest.

For family doctors, liberty prevails. They are mainly self-employed, can set up a private practice wherever they like, prescribe what they like, and are paid per consultation. The French visit the doctor more than twice as often as the Swedes and take, on average, more pills per person than any other country in the EU. The choice and freedom in the French health care system come at a price. The French public health fund deficit is steadily increasing and soared to over €12 billion (euros), approximately $16 billion, in 2005 according to the Health Ministry. This deficit is expected to rise to €29 billion by 2010.

France is facing the rising cost of drug spending like any other rich country. So what is the solution? Hiking the contribution of 'sociale generalisee,' a widely based revenue tax, would fill the financing gap. A rise of just one percentage point would bring in some €10 billion. Other solutions are also being considered, including the dispersal of only drugs that really are useful. The Health Ministry has set up an authority to study various options in order to reduce the cost of pharmaceutical spending.

# Germany

Germany is Europe's largest economy, and it is the fourth largest economy in the world. It is also the most populous country among European Community (EU) countries. The Federal Republic of Germany has a mixed system of socialized and private health care, which covers virtually all the residents within its borders. In some ways, it is a two-tier health care system. The German health care system has the reputation of being one of the best in the world. There is an extensive network of hospitals and doctors covering even the most remote areas of Germany.

## General information

Germany has a land area of 357,021 Sq km, which is slightly smaller than Montana. The Allied Powers formed the two German states in 1949 soon after World War II—in the west, the Federal Republic of Germany (FRG) and in the east, the German Democratic Republic (GDR). The end of the Cold War allowed German unification in 1990. The Federal Republic of Germany had a booming economy from 1949 until the unification, but German economic growth has been sluggish since then. Germany is the founding member of the European Economic Community (EEC), now called the European Union (EU).

## Other statistics

The population of Germany was 82,369,552 in July of 2008, consisting of 91.5% German, 2.4% Turks, and 6.1% 'others' (Serbo-Croatian, Polish, Russian, Italian, Greek, Spanish, and Asian). Germany absorbed over 15 million people from East Germany after the fall of the Berlin Wall. The population growth rate was almost zero despite net immigration 2.19 migrants per thousand of the population.

The gross domestic product (GDP) per person was equivalent to $34,100 and unemployment was nearly 9% in 2007. The literacy rate was nearly 100%. With the reunification of Germany, the East

German mark converted, in a one to one ratio, to the West German mark. The conversion has led to sluggish growth in the German economy and has produced high unemployment rates.

The median age of the population was 43.4 years and the infant mortality rate was 4.03 deaths per thousand live births in 2005. The average life expectancy was 79.1 years. Male life expectancy was 76.1 years while that of females was 82.26 years.

The unemployment rate among the people living in eastern Germany and among minorities was substantially higher than that of the people that lived in the western part of Germany.

## Health care system

*Health care spending accounted for 10.6% of Germany's GDP for the year 2006, according to the OECD. This figure was adjusted for purchasing-power parity, including both public and private spending.*

The German health care system has evolved over the last hundred years, with different types of workers brought into the state health insurance system. After World War II, the German constitution incorporated the Basic Law of 1949. According to this law, the federal government has exclusive authority in public health insurance matters and sets broad health care policy. Statutory health insurance, called Gesetzliche Krankenversicherung (GKV), provides an organizational framework for the delivery of health care to the public.

The right to health care is sacred in Germany. All political parties endorse universal coverage, comprehensive benefits, the principle of the healthy paying for the sick, and a redistributive element in the financing of health care. The Basic Law secures these rights and principles.

The federal government shapes the policies particular to benefits, eligibility, compulsory membership, covered risks (physical, emotional, mental, curative, and preventive), and income maintenance during temporary illness. It also regulates employer-employee contributions to GKV (also called Krankenkassen). However, the government delegates responsibility for administering and delivering health care to non-state entities, which include national and regional associations of health care providers, *Land (state)* hospital associations, non-profit insurance funds, private insurance companies, and voluntary organizations. Individuals can carry their medical card to any part of Germany. No one in need of care can be turned away without running the risk of violating the codes of medical ethics (known as *Land* hospital laws).

Most residents in Germany receive health care coverage through the state health insurance plan funded from contributions to the GKV, based on a network of hundreds of nonprofit 'sickness funds' (Krankassen), which have nearly the same role that health insurance provider's play in the United States. Membership in the statutory health insurance system is compulsory for employed people up to a certain income. The self-employed and the more affluent can take out private insurance. The government pays the cost of Krankenkassen membership for the unemployed, welfare recipients, students, and some other groups as determined by the state. Revenues generated from membership fees pay for the services of health care providers.

**Health insurance**

Over 90% of Germany's residents receive health care through compulsory health insurances. Salaried employees earning more than the income limit (decided by the state) can either purchase private health insurance, or enroll in the state insurance program. The average general health insurance contribution rate was nearly 14% of the non-exempt portion of employees' income in 2003. Employees and employers each paid half of the contributions. People earning below €480 per month (an amount decided yearly by the state) are required to pay less towards their insurance. The state provides subsidy insurance for the poor, the unemployed, students and the elderly. Only a quarter of the people with incomes above the limit choose to purchase private health insurance.

Private health insurance was nearly 12% of Germany's total health expenditure in 2003. A person covered by statutory health insurance automatically has long-term insurance care too. Premiums are set according to earnings, rather than risk. Marital status, family size, and state of health do not affect them. They are the same for all members of a particular fund with the same earnings. Some sickness-fund members buy additional private insurance to secure extras, such as a private room, or a choice of physicians while in hospital.

Members of the statutory insurance plan have to pay the equivalent of $10 to $20, as an additional contribution for various health care services, due to government reforms put into practice on January 1, 2004. Some people were exempt from these payments, including children under eighteen years old, the poor, the unemployed, war victims, students, and the disabled.

## Health care providers

The principal health care providers are physicians, dentists, and three types of hospitals: public, private non-profit, and private for-profit. The health industry also includes large pharmaceutical companies and the manufacturers of various kinds of medical supplies. There are two types of physicians:

- Those who provide office-based or ambulatory care for their patients; office-based physicians are fee-for-service doctors whose incomes depend on the amount and type of medical care they provide. A patient can only go to the hospital when referred by an office-based physician, or in the case of an emergency.

- Those who provide medical care at the hospitals; hospital physicians are mainly salaried employees of the hospitals where they work. When a patient leaves the hospital, he or she again comes under the care of an office-based physician.

Regional state governments, municipalities, and counties own most of the public sector hospitals. They provide about 50% of all hospital beds. Catholic or Protestant organizations typically run non-profit hospitals. They provide about 35% of the beds. For-profit hospitals account for 15%.

There is no separation between hospitalization and medical benefits. These benefits are uniform, with only minor variations among insurance plans. Krankenkasse members and their families may choose their own doctors and dentists. Some doctors may only accept private patients. When residents in Germany go to a doctor, they present a card instead of paying directly. Office-based, hospital doctors, and dentists, bill the insurance company directly for all the services rendered to a particular patient within a given quarter. Coverage includes all professional consultations, examinations, surgery, therapy, convalescence, and home nursing. Co-payments are required for pharmaceuticals, acute hospital care, and dental work. The statutory insurance plan provides insured people with 80% of their normal salary if their employer does not continue to pay them while they are absent from work due to illness.

## Remunerations of heath care providers

There are yearly negotiations and agreements between the national association of sickness funds and the national association of physicians. Similar bargaining procedures apply to dental care. The associations work within guidelines suggested by the Advisory Council for Concerted Action in Health Care, and establish agreements on guidelines for the delivery of medical care and fee schedules tied to the relative scales of about 2,000 medical procedures. At the national level, the Federal Committee of Sickness Funds Physicians and Sickness Funds is a key player. It sets spending limits on the practice of medicine in physicians' offices, determines the inclusion of new medical procedures and preventive services, and adjusts remunerations for physicians and dentists. It also formulates guidelines on the distribution and joint use of sophisticated medical technology and equipment by ambulatory-care or office based physicians, and hospital physicians.

At the regional level, associations negotiate specific contracts, including overall health budgets, reimbursement contracts for physicians in the region, the procedure for monitoring physicians, and the reference standard for prescription drugs.

Sickness-funds transfer monies amounting to the negotiated budget for the region, to the regional sickness-fund associations. The associations then pay their members based on points earned from services performed during the billing period. The negotiated fee-for services schedule, which assigns points to each service according to a relative value scale, determines the cost of services. No exchange of money occurs between sickness-fund patients and physicians. Privately insured patients pay their physicians themselves and their insurance companies then reimburse them.

To prevent physicians from attempting to earn more via increased billing for unnecessary services, committees of doctors and sickness funds closely scrutinize physician practices. There are penalties for physicians found guilty of improper conduct. The same procedures apply to dentists as well.

*Land* hospital associations and *Land* sickness-fund associations negotiate the general standard for hospital care and procedures, and determine the criteria by which to monitor the appropriate and efficient delivery of medical care. Each hospital negotiates a contract on hospital care, and the prices for hospital services, with regional sickness-fund associations. *Land* general revenues finance hospital investments and equipment.

Like any other rich country, the cost of health care is outpacing inflation and the ever-increasing age of the population. The challenge in Germany is to accelerate the use of preventive health care, to educate its population on healthy eating habits, the benefits of exercise, moderate consumption of alcohol, and to restrict smoking.

# India

India, like Cuba, is not one of the rich industrialized nations, but it is included for two reasons. One, because it is an example of a highly privatized health care system, and two, because its biotech and IT industries, as well as it's highly trained medical professionals, have much to offer in the search for solutions to universal and affordable health care.

India achieved its independence from British rule in 1947, after Mohandas Gandhi and Jawaharlal Nehru led nonviolent resistance to British colonization. The old India was split into two countries, Muslim Pakistan and secular India. Nehru became the first Prime Minister of an India that followed a mostly non-aligned foreign policy, and a state controlled economy. Only in the last two decades has the economy slowly been released from state and bureaucratic controls towards a market economy.

For nearly a decade, India has been one of the fastest growing economies in the world, achieving growth rates of 7–8% a year. Note that it started with a very low gross domestic product (GDP) base though. In 2007, the rate was just below 8%.

India has developed a large infrastructure in primary health care in rural and urban areas. Health care facilities increased substantially between the early 1950s and early 1980s, but because of rapid population growth, the number of licensed medical practitioners per every 10,000 individuals had fallen by late 1980s.

## General information

India has a land area of 3,287,590 Sq km, which is slightly more than one-third the size of the United States. The country, bordered by Pakistan, China, Bangladesh, Bhutan, and Nepal, is located in Southeast Asia. Parts of the Arabian Sea, Indian Ocean, and the Bay of Bengal also surround India.

The population of India was estimated to be 1,147, 996,000 by July of 2007, and consisted of 80% Hindus, 13.5% Muslims, 2.3% Christians, 1.9% Sikhs, and a small fraction of 'others.' Hindi is the national language spoken by around 30% of the population. There are fourteen other official languages. English enjoys an associate status, and is the language widely used for national, political, and commercial communication.

India is the largest democracy in the world. The central government devolves power to twenty-eight states and seven union territories.

## A little history

The Indian Subcontinent people are from an old culture. Aryan tribes infiltrated into the subcontinent about 1500 B.C., and then merged with earlier Dravidian inhabitants. This created the classical Indian culture. The Mauryan Empire of the third and fourth centuries B.C. reached its peak under king Ashoka, who united much of South Asia. The golden age ushered in by the Gupta Dynasty (400–600 A. D.) saw advancements in Indian sciences. Arab incursions started in the eighth century, leading to Mogul rulers, followed by the intrusion of European traders in the beginning of late fifteenth century. By the nineteenth century, Britain, assisted by local rulers, had assumed political control of the Indian subcontinent completely. Indian armed forces in the British Army played a vital role in both world wars.

A war between India and Pakistan in 1971 resulted in East Pakistan becoming the separate nation of Bangladesh. India tested nuclear device in 1998, and has run an independent foreign policy. Only in the last twenty years has the government of India allowed an open market economy, which has lead to impressive growth rates.

Despite these gains in economic investment and output, India faces the pressing problems of over population, environmental degradation, extensive poverty, poor infrastructure, and to an extent, ethnic and religious strife.

## Other statistics

In 2006, the GDP per person estimate was equivalent to $3,800, with an unemployment rate of 7.8% and an economic growth rate of 9.6% in 2007.

The literacy rate was 61%. The median age of the population was around 24.8 years, while the infant mortality rate was 34.61 per thousand. Average life expectancy was 69.25 years. For males, it was 66.87 years and for females, it was 71.9 years, in June 2008.

## Health care system

The central government may set the policy guidelines for health care in conjunction with the states and territories, but the states and territories administer their own health care systems without any interference from the central government.

India has one of the most privatized medical systems in the world, with the government meeting only 17% of total health care costs, compared to 47% in the United States and about 92% in the United Kingdom. The government annual per capita expenditure on health care is only $4.00. There is an urgent need for the government to increase health care expenditure as a percentage of GDP to 5% from the 2007 low of 3%. (*Improving India's Public Health System*, August 2, 2007)

Dr. Arnold Relman, Professor Emeritus of Medicine and Social Medicine, Harvard School of Medicine and author of the book, *A Second Opinion: Rescuing America's Health Care*, delivered a keynote speech at a forum jointly organized by the Asia Society and the Observer Research Foundation in New York in November 2007. In it, he stated:

> The best advice that I can give India is to ignore the sales pitch of those who promote privatization with the false claim that it is the best route to a more affordable and accessible health system. Do not follow the path taken by the U.S. over the past few decades. Instead, learn from the many mistakes we have made.

He went on to say, "To understand these mistakes and appreciate the lessons that India should draw, we need to look closely at the U.S. health care system."

Over the past six decades since independence in 1947, India has developed a large infrastructure for primary health care in rural and urban areas. This infrastructure includes Community Health Centers (CHC), Primary Health Centers (PHC), sub-centers, and district hospitals. Paramedics and doctors staff almost all the infrastructure in rural and urban areas. At the state and central level, doctors and general administrators manage the PHC infrastructure.

The health care system in India is pluralistic, meaning that there are many different kinds of practitioners, in different settings, with different ideological beliefs about disease control and prevention. It is not regulated strictly at the state level. There are magic/religious cures of priests and other religious institutions as well as home and herbal remedies, all of which may be considered too extreme in terms of western medical practices.

Traditional medical practitioners continue to practice throughout the country. The two main forms of traditional medicine are the *ayurvedic* (meaning science of life) system that deals with causes, symptoms, diagnoses, and treatment based on all aspects of well-being (mental, physical, and spiritual), and *unani* (so-called *'Galenic'* medicine) the practice of herbal medicine. A *vaidya* is a practitioner of the ayurvedic tradition, while a *hakim* (Arabic for a Muslim physician) is a practitioner of the unani tradition. In the mid 1990s, there were over 100 ayurvedic colleges and 20 unani colleges operating in public and private sectors.

The following table gives a rough understanding of the scale of government health care infrastructure in India.

Figure 8

| Level of health facility | Number of institutions 1997* | Number of institutions 2007** |
|---|---|---|
| Medical college hospitals | 150 | 300 |
| District hospitals | 400 | 800 |
| Community Health Centers (CHC) | 3,000 | 5,000 |
| Primary Health Centers (PHC) | 20,000 | 35,000 |
| Sub-centers (SC) | 130,000 | 200,000 |

Note: 1997* figures are rough for the scale of health care infrastructure, while 2007** figures were projected.
Source: Medical Council of India (MCI)1997

There is a lack of professional management training at any level in the PHC system. The health department hierarchy in some states, such as Gujarat and Maharashtra, mandates training for district level and higher officers, in public health. Most doctors in charge of clinical facilities such as CHCs, rural hospitals, and district hospitals, are MBBS doctors or clinical specialists with little or no training in management. One of the reasons for the sub-optimal results in the health sector and family planning programs is the lack of appropriate management input. In recent years, more stress has been placed on learning management skills in the undergraduate curriculum established by the MCI.

As mentioned earlier, India has one of the most privatized medical systems in the world, where the private sector meets 83% of total health care costs. There is a huge private health care system, which includes health care workers, doctors, hospitals and clinics, as well as practitioners of every other aspect of medicine, from allopathic, homeopathic, acupuncture, and herbal medicine, to magic/religious cures etc.

The health models that can work in India can serve as a guide for the rest of the world according to Ron Summers, President of the U.S. - India Business Council (USIBC). India offers good opportunities for USIBC-member companies to take part in providing better health care for the country's population. There are tremendous possibilities for lowering the cost of drugs, hence the cost of treatment. There is already a developing medical tourism industry, which treats Americans in Indian institutions, for about one tenth of the cost in the U.S. Chapter 6 covers these points in detail, as they relate to the American health care system.

# Japan

Japan experienced unprecedented economic growth for three decades. Since 1990 economic growth has either been sluggish or in recession, and the Japanese economy has experienced a major slow down. This has mainly been due to bad loans accumulated by Japanese banks, and the bursting of the property bubble in the early 1990s.

In 1961, Japanese established health insurance for all its citizens, enabling anyone to afford necessary medical care. Japan practices a universal health care insurance system in which all the residents subscribe to one of the medical care insurance systems, so that everybody has access to adequate medical care without worries.

## General information

Japan has a land area of 377,835 Sq km, which is slightly smaller than California. During the late nineteenth and early twentieth centuries, Japan became a regional power. It occupied Korea, Taiwan, and parts of China and Russia. Japanese forces attacked the United States of America in 1941, triggering America's entry into World War II. After the surrender of Japan in 1945, America assisted Japan in building its economy. Today it is the second largest economy in the world.

## Other statistics

The population of Japan was 127,288,416 in July 2008, consisting of 99% Japanese, 1% 'others' (mainly Korean, Chinese, and Filipinos). Japanese society is almost homogeneous. The net migration rate for Japan was zero.

The gross domestic product (GDP) per person was equivalent to $33,500, according to 2008 estimates. The unemployment rate was 4.5%. The average economy grew by 10% in the 1960s, 5% in the 1970s, and 4% in the 1980s. The Japanese economy began to grow in the 1–2% range in the last few years, with almost zero inflation in the economy. The literacy rate was nearly 100%.

The median age of the population was 43.8 years in 2008, and the infant mortality rate was 2.8 deaths per thousand live births. The average life expectancy was 82.07 years. For males, life expectancy was 78.73 years, while it was 85.59 for females. The Japanese have one of the longest life expectancies in the world.

The percentage of Japanese men who smoke is much higher, in comparison, to their counterparts in Western Europe and America.

## Health care system

*In 2006, Japan spent 8.2% of its GDP per person on health care, which included both public and private contributions, according to the OECD. In comparison, the estimated American health care expenditure was nearly 15.3% of its GDP in 2006.*

Japan has a system of universal health care coverage for all its citizens, established in 1961. The Ministry of Health and Care Services, Labour, and Welfare is responsible for the health care system. The Minister's Secretariat supervises the administration of the Ministry, and takes charge of comprehensive coordination, including drafting of basic policies, amendments to, and abolition of laws and ordinances, compilation of the budget, organization, and personnel affairs. Over the years, there has been steady evolvement of policies and laws governing health care.

## Structure and organization

*The Minister's Secretariat* is the core organization for comprehensive coordination within the ministry and represents the whole ministry at the Diet (the Japanese parliament), or, towards other ministries and agencies, mass media, and the population at large. There are several bureaus relating to health care, which perform different functions under the Secretariat. These bureaus include:

- Health Policy Bureau

- Health Service Bureau, which also includes the Department of National Hospitals

- Pharmaceutical and Food Safety Bureau

- Department of Health and Welfare for Persons with Disability

- Health and Welfare Bureau for the Elderly

- Health Insurance Bureau

*The Health Policy Bureau* thinks of medical services for tomorrow. It plans and proposes policies for developing an effective system offering medical services in the twenty-first century, in response to the aging of the population, changes in disease structure, and stronger demands for medical services of higher quality. The bureau strives to create a medical system wherein citizens receive stress free, high-quality medical services when they are ill or injured. It also actively promotes information on medical services and the development of new techniques and new drugs to the citizens.

*The Health Service Bureau* aims to overcome diseases and enhance health. It acts to improve health through centers that take steps against infectious diseases, such as Ebola hemorrhagic fever, AIDS, and tuberculosis, and diseases caused by lifestyle, such as diabetes and cancer, while also promoting appropriate organ transplants. In short, the bureau aims to improve the health of each Japanese national. It also strives to secure a comfortable and sanitary daily living environment, as well as formulating and then implementing policies for organ transplantation.

*The Department of National Hospitals* is part of the Health Service Bureau. This department operates an established, policy based, medical services network. It takes charge of the operation of nearly 220 national hospitals and sanatoriums (private and public), and the National Center for Advanced and Specialized Medical Care.

National hospitals and sanatoriums are mainly engaged in the following activities:

- Advanced frontier medical care: This involves organ transplantation from brain-dead bodies, and radiotherapy of cancers.

- Those providing medical care not easily provided on the regional level, or by the private sector, due to historical, social, or other backgrounds: National sanatoriums treat almost all Hansen's disease patients, over 80% of those with

Muscular Dystrophy, as well as around 50% of all people with severe mental and physical disabilities.

- Those implementing important medical policies from an international point of view: Providing assessment of risk management along with the dispatch of doctors and nurses to hot spots where medical care is required.

The implementation of reforms will reorganize national hospitals and sanatoriums into independent administrative corporations.

*The Pharmaceutical and Medical Safety Bureau* oversees the safety of drugs and medical care for patients. The bureau implements measures to secure the effectiveness and safety of drugs, cosmetics, and medical services. It also ensures safety measures in medical institutions, sets standards for narcotics and stimulants, handles the safe blood donation and transfusion business, and promotes a variety of measures for the eradication of drug and stimulant abuse.

*The Department of Health and Welfare for Persons with Disabilities* works towards the independence and social participation of the disabled. This department aims to create a society in which people, with and without disability, help one another live in a community promoting vitality. In short, the department encourages policies that lead to normalization of life for people with disabilities. It secures medical care for people with mental diseases, as well as providing resources and the training of volunteers who are capable of sign language and braille, in order to improve the quality of life for the disabled. Disabled people living at home receive welfare services.

*The Health and Welfare Bureau for the Elderly* aims to create a society in which aged people can live a healthy life, with peace of mind. It is expected that one in three Japanese people will be sixty-five years and older by the middle of the twenty-first century. All municipalities in Japan have created a unified health and welfare insurance plan for the elderly, which incorporates long-term care.

*The Health Insurance Bureau* provides health care for all people. The Japanese health care system is highly regulated. The system combines a mainly private provision of services with mandatory health insurance, regulated by the Health Insurance Bureau. There are two types of health insurance and all people are assigned to a health insurer according to their employment situation. The Social Insurance System (SIS) insures those employed by a company or office. Employers, who pay 50–80% of the cost, fund this system as well as premiums paid by the employees. The National Health Insurance (NHI) insures the rest, including the unemployed, the elderly, the self-employed, and employees of the SIS. There are hundreds of health insurance societies across the nation, which are part of the SIS. The premiums depend on the employee's annual income, but amount to approximately 8.5%. An insured person and his or her dependents must make a small contribution to outpatient costs, and make co-payments for prescription drugs. Premiums for people covered by NHI depend on income, assets, and benefit payments from the previous year.

A third type of insurance, started in April 2000, helps to cope with the aging population. Users of this insurance, half funded by health insurance, and half by individuals aged forty or older; also enroll in mandatory insurance plans.

The law requires health insurers to offer a basic package of benefits, which includes medical consultation, drugs, medical treatment and surgery, home care treatment and nursing, hospitalization and nursing at medical institutions, and other health care services.

## Health care expenditure

Japanese health care providers are predominately, private hospitals and physicians. By law, hospitals must operate as non-profit entities. Hospitals are the most important providers of health care, and constitute nearly 90% of health care services. About 80% of hospitals are private, physician-owned, and 20% are large public, state owned, teaching hospitals. Salaried physicians staff public and private hospitals. Private physicians practice and treat patients in offices or clinics, and do not have hospital medical staff privileges. Both hospitals and clinics treat patients, who have the right to choose where they want to go for treatment.

All doctors and physicians receive the same fee for each service. Almost all doctors in private clinics try to deal with all the problems of their patients. The fee for a given service is identical across service providers.

## Remunerations for health care services

Doctors, physicians, medical practitioners with their own offices, hospitals, and pharmacies receive partial payments from patients (usually around 14%) for the medical treatment rendered and prescription medicine dispensed. The patients' health insurance plans provide the rest of the payment. There is a standard rate on medicines, fixed by the appropriate bureau. The rates for each type of health care service, including seeing a doctor, or any type of procedure or surgery performed by a physician or in hospital, are also fixed. In other words, the rate depends on the content of the treatment. A system that assigns a specified number of points to the type of treatment and medicine provided calculates an official piece rate for payments.

## Challenges

Japan has one of the lowest health care costs per person of the world's rich countries, yet the average life expectancy is one of the highest and the infant mortality rate is one of the lowest. The main reason for the low cost of health care is the homogeneity of the Japanese society, and the fact that people tend to follow established rules in health care services. Fraud and malpractice lawsuits are almost negligible in the Japanese health care system.

Nearly 55% of Japanese men smoke, which is the number one preventable cause of death in the country. The government faces challenges in keeping the cost of health care from rising sharply as the society ages. One in three people will be sixty-five and over by the year 2050, the largest percentage of elderly people in any society in the world. There is also the challenge of mounting an aggressive campaign persuading people to cut down on smoking.

The Japanese people are traditionally unwilling to voice displeasure with government health care policies. The rising cost of health care is causing an increasing number of people to speak out. They are becoming more sensitive to the quality of health care, long waiting times for outpatient service in large hospitals, frequent reporting of medical errors, and extremely short consultation times with their doctors.

The current strain on the health care system calls for the reform of various insurance plans, the medical fee schedule, and the prescription drug pricing system. There is also a need for improvement in long-term care. All of these challenges exist to a varying degree, in other countries as well.

# Norway

Norway has the highest per capita income (apart from Luxemburg) and low-income equality. The country is a constitutional monarchy governed by a three-tiered parliamentary system, elected by the populace. The three-tier body is the national parliament (Stortinget), the county council (Fylkestinget) and the municipal councils (Kommunestyret). The representatives for each body are elected for a four-year period by proportional representation.

Norway is the third largest exporter of oil and gas in the world, after Saudi Arabia and Russia. The country has been saving its oil-boosted budget surpluses in a government Petroleum Fund, which is valued at more than $150 billion. The Norwegian economy is a bastion of welfare capitalism, which is a combination of free market economy and government intervention.

The Norwegian health care system is publicly tax-financed, which is akin to the health care systems of other Nordic countries, and of the United Kingdom. This approach contrasts with the dominant model in many OECD countries, whereby a mix of public and private insurance provides funds for many privately provided services. The Norwegian health care system is universal, based on a person's need rather than the ability to pay, and covers all the population. Many consider it one of the finest health care systems in the world.

## General information

Norway has a land area of 324,220 sq km, which is slightly larger than New Mexico. It was absorbed into a union with Denmark, which lasted for more than four centuries. In 1814, Norwegians resisted the annexation of their country to Sweden. The country gained its independence in 1905 after a referendum. The Norwegians rejected joining the EU in a referendum in 1972, and again in1994. Norway has been a member of NATO since 1949.

## Other statistics

The population of Norway was 4,644,457 in July 2008, which included about 20,000 indigenous Sámi people, others from Scandinavian countries, and a small number of foreign-born people. The growth rate of the population was 0.4 % and net migration was 1.71 per thousand of the population. The infant mortality rate was 3.61 deaths per every thousand live births. The median age was 39.0 years, and the average life expectancy was 79.91 years. For males, life expectancy was 77.16 years, while it was 82.6 years for females. The literacy rate was 100%.

The gross domestic product estimate was equivalent to $53,300 in purchasing power parity in 2008. The unemployment rate was around 2.5%, and the population below poverty line was almost zero. The GDP growth picked up to 4.3% in 2004 after lackluster growth in the years 2002 and 2003, while it was 2.5% in 2007.

## Health care system

*Health care spending accounted for 8.7% of Norway's GDP for the year 2006, according to the OECD. This figure was adjusted for purchasing-power parity.*

The public health care services come under the jurisdiction of the Royal Norwegian Ministry of Health and Care Services, which is responsible for devising and monitoring national health policy. There was a gradual emergence of the welfare state during the 1900s, accompanied by a major expansion of the Norwegian health care system.

After World War II, Norway developed a system for health care built on the principle of universality. All inhabitants have the same access to quality, publicly funded health care services independent of social status, location, and income. People who fall ill in Norway are guaranteed medical treatment. The health care system is a cornerstone of the Norwegian welfare state. The responsibility for delivery of health care is decentralized to municipal and county councils. The municipalities are responsible for primary health care, as well as general practitioner clinics, while hospitals come under the direct responsibility of the central government.

Patient's fees for doctors, specialists, psychologists, and other health providers, are limited—no one pays more than about 1,500 kr (Norwegian kroner), which is about $200 a year. The government caps fees and patients are reimbursed if they spend more than that. Doctors and other health providers receive subsidies from municipal and county administrations. Prescription medicines, medical equipment, and treatment at private x-ray clinics, are also virtually free for patients. All treatment provided during hospitalization is free of charge.

The Norwegian health care system is known for extensive coverage, high quality, and proven medical competence. Over 95% of the population expressed satisfaction with the professional skills of their physicians, and over 80% of those polled gave a positive approval of the results of treatment and the service attitude of medical staff.

**Health care spending and financing**

Norwegian health care is almost entirely publicly funded, with the private sector providing less than 1% of the total number of hospital beds and about 5% of outpatient services. The private clinics specialize in open-heart surgery, hip surgery, as well as minor surgeries.

The main sources of funding for these health care services are:

- Tax at the local level

- Transfer of funds from the central government

- The National Insurance Fund

- An obligatory user fee from patients for medical consultation

The central government provides grants to municipalities and counties, which in turn fund the primary health care system. Health care funding is a combination of general and separate taxation. National insurance, or social security, is a collective insurance scheme to which all the residents in Norway belong. Every wage earner contributes a fixed percentage of his or her earnings by paying the national insurance tax. In addition, employers contribute by means of payroll tax. The self-employed contribute more to social security than wage earners do, because they are exempt from payroll tax. The unemployed, non-working spouses, students and other without wages, are exempt from social security tax but they still qualify for all social security and health care benefits.

**Organizational structure of health care**

The Minister of Health and Care Services is responsible for promoting health policy, public health care, health care service providers, and health related legislation in Norway. His staff includes the State Secretaries and a political advisor. The Secretary General is responsible for the administrative management of the ministry and also oversees the Press and Information Unit, the Secretarial Office, and the political leadership.

The Ministry of Health and Care Services, consists of seven departments, each headed by a director general:

- The Department of Public Health

- Department of Municipal Health Care Services

- Department of Specialist Health Care Services

- The Department of Hospital ownership

- The Department of Health Legislation

- The Department of Administration

- The Department of Financial Affairs

These departments have subordinate institutions, one of which is the Patient Ombudsman. The Ombudsman reviews patient complaints and provides a system of compensation to patients, settling all matters concerning patient claims. It is very rare that any patient takes his or her claim directly to the courts.

The key areas of responsibility of the ministry are as follows:

- The public health system promotes prolonged healthy lives of the population by reducing the risk of contracting diseases, and reduced social inequality as far as health is concerned. It encourages physical activity and the prevention of the use of tobacco, and the use of addictive drugs. The ministry is also responsible for the realization of healthy and wholesome nutrition, and securing a safe food supply. The State also encourages a physical checkup for people over forty years old, which is free of charge.

- The primary health care system is the task of municipalities, in order to secure adequate and efficient medical treatment where people live. General practitioners, emergency clinics, and mother and child clinics, form a vital component of this service.

- Specialized services, including hospitals, out patient clinics, and ambulance services etc., primarily offer the population specialized medical treatment. These services are organized through five regional health authorities owned by the State, under the Ministry of Health and Care Services. The regional health authorities are responsible for providing specialized health care to the population, either through health care enterprises owned by the regional authority, or through a contract with private health care service providers.

- The public dental service covers only certain groups of the population. Dental care for these groups is free. The majority of the population is obliged to pay for these services themselves. The dental service is, however, responsible for securing equal accessibility to dental services to all age groups within all parts of the country.

- Support for those suffering from psychiatric disorders is given partly through primary health care, partly through specialized health care services, and through municipal and voluntary services not included in the health care system.

- Health care services to drug addicts are part of the ordinary health care service, which comprises of high accessibility to medical treatment, supported by medication. The responsibility for this specialized treatment is in the hands of state owned health authorities.

The pharmaceutical service is private in Norway, but the State regulates the cost of drugs. The public health care system secures reliable and safe access to medicine and makes it easily available to the population at a nominal price. Through the 'Blue Prescription' arrangement, the National Insurance System grants financial support to patients with special needs.

Alternative medical treatment, such as acupuncture and homeopathy, was not part of the public health care system in 2005; however, alternative medical treatment is available and is likely to become part of the health care system in Norway.

There are regulations on the use of biotechnology. Legislation and ethical questions related to biotechnology are the prime responsibility of the ministry.

The details of the Royal Norwegian Ministry of Health and Care Services and the ministry's subordinate institutions can be viewed at the ministry's website.

## Health service providers

The public health care sector is one of the largest in Norwegian society, employing nearly 230,000 people. There are nearly 280 per doctor. Doctors, otherwise known as general practitioners (GPs), and other health care providers employed by the municipality receive a centrally negotiated fixed salary. Municipalities employ 40% of the GPs. The GPs who run private practices under contracts with the municipality (50%) receive an annual grant. The State pays all hospital staff.

## Treatment abroad

The National Insurance Scheme (NIS) fully reimburses all individual expenses for childbirth and treatment of industrial injury. Private health insurance covering specific categories of individuals, or groups, for special surgery or treatment is virtually non-existent in Norway. If a patient's ailment is potentially fatal or unusual, and Norwegian hospitals lack the professional competence for treatment, social security covers the cost of treatment abroad. Other Scandinavian countries and Germany provide any specialized treatment not available in Norway. Local hospitals are responsible for selecting these patients, as well as for asking whether the patients are willing to travel abroad.

The Norwegian population is also covered for treatment and medication if they develop any sickness or illness while traveling abroad on holiday or business. Residents of the other EU countries can receive free medical health care, in an emergency, while traveling in Norway as well.

## Challenges

The population of Norway is growing older. In particular, the oldest segment of the population is expanding, as in the other rich countries of Europe, and this represents an extra burden on the health care system. Mental illness is on the rise, with more people committing suicide, especially younger people and men over eighty years old, than in other countries in the EU. The Norwegian Foreign Ministry claims that the suicide rate has stabilized.


# Spain

Spain's powerful world empire of the sixteenth and seventeenth centuries ultimately yielded to the command of the seas by England. Spain remained neutral in World War I and II, but suffered through a devastating civil war (1936–39). Spain joined the European Union (EU) in 1986, and is now in the Euro-zone. Spain is also a member of NATO.

Spain's public health care system has been evolving since 1885. The country has developed a comprehensive system of public health care that has assumed more responsibility since the beginning of the last century. After the death of Dictator General Franco in 1975, the country returned to a parliamentary democracy. Article 43 of the Spanish Constitution of 1978 established not only a constitutional monarchy, but also the premise of health care.

## General information

Spain has a land area of 504,782 Sq Km, which is slightly more than twice the size of Oregon, and is the third largest country in Western Europe. There are nineteen autonomous regions, including the Balearic and Canary Islands.

## Other statistics

The population of Spain was 40,491,052 in July 2008. This also included people from Morocco, who primarily live in the Canary Islands. The growth rate of the population was 0.15%, while net migration was 0.99 per thousand people. The median age was 40.7 years. The infant mortality rate before the age of one was 4.26 deaths per every thousand births. The average life expectancy was 79.92. For males, life expectancy was 76.6 years while it was 83.45 years for females. The literacy rate was 97.9%.

The gross domestic product (GDP) per capita was equivalent to $33,600 in 2008. The Spanish economy boomed from 1986 to 1990 at an average annual growth rate of 5%. The annual growth rate was 2.5 % in 2003 and 2.6% in 2004 respectively, while the economy grew by 3.8% in 2007. The unemployment rate was 8.3%, which is high compared to other countries in the EU.

Spain successfully worked to gain admission to the first group of countries launching the European single currency (the Euro).

Spain is widely known for Flamenco music and dancing, bullfights, fantastic beaches and lots of sunshine.

## Health care system

*Health care spending accounted for 8.4% of Spain's GDP for the year 2006 according to the OECD. This figure was adjusted for purchasing-power parity.*

The health care system embodied in Article 43 of the Spanish Constitution of 1978 reads:

> The right to protection of health is recognized.
>
> It is incumbent upon the public authorities to organize and
> safeguard public health by means of preventive measures and necessary benefits and services. The law shall establish the rights
> and duties of all concerned in this respect.
>
> The public authorities shall foster health education, physical education, and sports. Likewise, they shall encourage the proper use of leisure.

Spain reconstructed the Ministry of Health and Care Services after the country returned to parliamentary democracy. Public health care organization, policy, and budget financing are the responsibility of the Ministry of Health and Care Services, while the National

Institute of Public Health Care (INSALUD) is responsible for the managerial functions of public health care.

The Spanish parliament passed the General Law of Public Health Care in 1986. This law created the right of the population to receive health care services free of charge at the point of delivery. Public insurance coverage of the population is over 99%. The Inter-territorial Council of the National Health System (ICNPHS) was set up in 1987. A number of different bodies such as State public administration, autonomous communities, local corporations, groups providing health services—doctors, hospital staff, and privately contracted people etc., later agreed to harmonize the health care policies of the State and the seventeen autonomous communities under ICNPHS.

The Spanish National Health Care System has a vast network of medical centers and hospitals spread across the country. They offer all primary care services, as well as specialized attention.

Autonomous communities and local authorities administer all health care services in their regions according to harmonized health care policies.

In January 2002, Spain devolved health care responsibilities to all seventeen regions for administrative purposes. Spanish residents have the right to enjoy similar quality health care services, and to be able get every prescription medicine, in all regions of Spain.

The Ministry of Health and Care Services created The National Plan on Drug Addiction in 1985 in an effort to tackle the complex phenomenon of drug addition at all levels. This comprehensive plan coordinated the activities of different departments of the State, the seventeen autonomous regions, local administrations, and a number of non-governmental organizations working with drug addicts.

**Funding of Spanish health care**

The Spanish health care sector is mainly public, both in terms of funding and in terms of delivery. Over 98% of the funding for health care comes from general taxation. Spain spends a relatively smaller amount on health care, as a percentage of GDP, than other countries in the OECD, yet the people enjoy parity with other rich countries in longevity and in living a healthy life.


**Private insurance and waiting lists**

Public health care services have a waiting list for non-urgent operations, and for seeing a specialist. In order to avoid the waiting times, a very small percentage of Spanish citizens insure themselves with private companies. Most resident foreigners also have private health care insurance. They must present either their social security card, evidence of private insurance, or proof of ability to pay the bills while attending a hospital, except in the case of emergency. On July 1, 2004, the European Union (EU) countries established the European Health Card. This card entitles all residents of EU countries medical care identical to that of the residents of any particular country within the EU. Private insurance is optional.

**Co-payments and cost of prescription medicine**

The Spanish government has focused on containing the cost of health care services, especially pharmaceutical expenditure. It has been reasonably successful in these polices over the last decade. The main instrument of limiting costs is through price control. The Ministry of Health and Care Services sets maximum prices for every individual medicine licensed and commercially distributed in the country. The government developed a criterion for calculating the price of each one. This is similar to cost control mechanisms of other EU countries.

Patient co-payments for prescription drugs are very nominal and are usually lower than co-payments in other EU countries are. Health care services are either free or at a very low cost to the patient.

**Challenges**

Spanish authorities face challenges in reducing waiting times for non-essential surgeries, as well as in containing health care costs. The waiting list problems are very similar to those of England.

In general, the Spanish enjoy longevity of life and good health comparable to other EU countries. The prime reasons for a healthy life in Spain are its temperate climate combined with the Mediterranean diet, which includes fish, olives, salads, and red wine.

# Sweden

Sweden has lived in peace since 1814, after constant wars in previous centuries. It has a mixed economy with a substantial welfare state. The country, known abroad for its high standard of living, has publicly financed systems of economic security for all people in all phases of life.

The provision of financing for the populations' health care system is a public sector responsibility, as in other Nordic countries, and the United Kingdom. The goal of the Swedish health care system is to provide equal access to health services for everyone in Sweden.

## General information

Sweden is a constitutional monarchy. Democratically elected members of parliament (Riksdag) hold office for a period that usually lasts for four years. There are also county councils and local authority (municipality) elections. Sweden distributes the fruits of economic success more evenly amongst the population. It is a member of the European Union (EU), but the Swedish people rejected the common European currency of the Euro in the referendum. It is not a member of NATO.

Sweden has a land area of 450,000 sq km, which is larger than California, and is one of the three largest countries in Western Europe.

## Other statistics

The population of Sweden was 9,045,389 in July 2008. It consisted of around 87% Swedes, small minorities of Finnish, indigenous Sámi people, and foreign born or first-generation immigrants from Finland, Norway, Denmark, Greece, Turkey, and old Yugoslavia. There were also small minorities of people born in Asia, Africa, and Arab countries who resided in Sweden. The population growth rate was 0.16%. There was a net migration of 1.66 migrants per thousand of the population. The median age was 41.3 years. Infant mortality rate was 2.75 deaths per thousand live births, which was the lowest figure in the world apart from Singapore. The average life expectancy was 80.74 years. For males, this was 78.49 years while it was 83.13 for females.

The GDP per person was equivalent to $37,500 in 2007. The unemployment rate was 6.1 %, and the economic growth rate was 2.7%. The literacy rate was almost 100% and the poverty rate was almost negligible.

## Health care system

*Health care spending accounted for 9.2% of Sweden's GDP for 2006, according to the OECD. This figure was adjusted for purchasing-power parity.*

Three political and administrative levels operate in Sweden: the central government, the county council, and the local authority (municipality).

The central government establishes basic principles for health care services through laws and ordinances. The most important of these is the Health and Medical Services Act of 1982, which states that people shall be offered health services of good quality that are on equal terms, and are easily accessible to all the population. The services provided shall respect the patient's integrity and his choice to make his own decisions. Other laws regulate the obligations and responsibilities of health care personnel, professional confidentiality, patient's records, and health profession qualifications. The Ministry of Health and Care Services and Social Affairs is responsible for health care issues.

The responsibility of administering health care lies primarily with the county councils, which operate almost all services and levies taxes to finance them. The health services in Sweden rest largely in the hands of local politicians in the different geographical areas.

## Health care spending and funding

The cost of health services in Sweden amounted to 178 billion kr (Swedish krona) in the year 2000. This figure included pharmaceutical preparations and dental care. Health care spending was 8.5% of the GDP in 2000, rising to 9.2% in 2002. Services financed and provided by the county councils accounted for 80% of the spending. The county councils are entitled to levy a proportional tax on the incomes of their residents (the average tax rate being 10%). The central government also makes grants and payments for health care services. Patients' fees amount to 4% of county council revenue.

In the late 1990s, it became increasingly common for county councils to put health care services out to tender. The amount of care supplied by private health care providers rose steadily from a very small percentage to almost 10% of total county council expenditure in 2002. Almost 30% of all visits to doctors take place at private medical establishments.

## Health services

The primary health care system is the level that people should be able to turn to with any health problem. Primary health care involves improving the general health of the population, and treating diseases and injuries that do not require hospitalization.

There are well-organized health centers, which employ a wide variety of health professionals including physicians, nurses, auxiliary nurses, midwives, and physiotherapists. All patients have the right to choose their own family doctor or general practitioner.

In addition to services available at local public health centers and doctor surgeries, private doctors and health professionals at district nurse surgeries and maternity and pediatric clinics provide primary health care as well. All children under school age can get free health checks, consultations, and treatments from the children's clinics, while expectant mothers receive free regular check-ups from midwives and doctors at the maternity clinics throughout their pregnancies. School health and occupational health services are also available. People in nursing homes and those living in service apartments have access to nursing services twenty-four hours a day.

County and regional levels provide treatment as well. County medical services offer psychiatric care. The regional medical system consists of hospitals offering a wide range of specialists. For example, they perform neurosurgery, thoracic surgery, and plastic surgery. They also have highly specialized laboratories.

**Fees paid by the patient[4]**

All residents of Sweden, regardless of nationality, are entitled to Swedish health care services at subsidized prices. Patients from EU/EEA countries (and some other countries with which Sweden has a special agreement) also receive emergency treatment at a subsidized rate.

Each county council sets its own fees for outpatient care. The fee for consulting a doctor in the primary health care services varies from 100 kr to 150 kr. The fee for consulting a hospital consultant or a doctor in a private practice ranges from 180 kr to 300 kr.

The fee charged for a hospital stay with treatment is 80 kr per day. The county council also sets patient fees for medical treatment provided by other health care professionals such as physiotherapists, occupational therapists, and nurses, and professionals, working in public health and private system. The fees vary from 50 kr to 100 kr per visit depending on the county council.

There is an upper cost ceiling for patients' fees. A patient who has paid a total of 900 kr (less than $120) in patient fees is entitled to free medical care for the rest of the twelve-month period, calculated

---

[4] *Source: The fees quoted are from the official site of SWEDEN.SE – Health Care System in Sweden, and are for the year 2000. The exchange rate was one dollar to 7.65 Swedish Krona (SEK) at that time.*

from the date of the first consultation. All medical treatment for children and young people under twenty is free of charge.

Sweden has an extensive system of benefits for the sick, the unemployed, and the disabled. The pensions and benefits for retired people are generous, and students receive extensive low interest loans for living expenses, or grants, during their time at college and other institutions of higher learning. There are no fees for college tuition.

## Dental care

The county councils are responsible for providing free dental care for children and young people up to the age of nineteen. Adults receive an economic subsidy from the national dental insurance system for basic dental care. Nearly half of all dentists work in the national dental service run by county councils, the others are private dentists.

The pricing for dental care has been deregulated, which means dentists set their own fees for each form of treatment. There is also an option to sign two-year agreements on the provision of basic dental care at a fixed price. There is a special high-cost protection system for those aged 65 or over for dental treatment, which is aimed at limiting the cost for the individual.

## Prescription drugs and cost

Sweden requires registration of all medicines sold in the country with the Medical Products Agency (Läkemedelsverket), which is the government authority responsible for the control of pharmaceutical preparations. Laws adapted to EU regulations, which govern medical products, regulate the activities of this authority. The Pharmaceutical Benefits Board (Läkemedelsformansnamnden) decides which pharmaceuticals are subsidized and how much they should cost. Negotiations with the manufacturer settle the price of a drug.

The patient pays the entire cost of the prescribed medicine up to 900 kr. Above this figure, a rising scale of subsidy operates, with a high-cost ceiling, meaning that the patient never has to pay more than 1,800 kr in any twelve-month period.

The state-owned National Corporation of Swedish Pharmacies (Apoteket AB) began privatization in 2009. It has the exclusive right to sell medicine to the public and to hospitals. The pharmaceutical companies have insurance coverage that provides compensation for patients whose health a medical drug damages.

**Heath care service providers**

The county council health services employ nearly 240,000 people, which is about 7% of the Swedish workforce. There was 1 physician to 320 inhabitants in the year 2000. The average salary of a hospital doctor with a specialist qualification was 46,000 kr ($6,013) per month, and the average salary of a nurse was 22,000 kr ($2,876) per month. The head of a department is, almost without exception, a medical doctor with the overall responsibility for medical care as well as administration, finance and staff.

Doctors are trained at the universities of Stockholm (Karolinska Institute), Gothenburg, Lund, Linköping, Uppsala and Umeå. Doctors are trained in an integrated manner within the operation of the university hospitals and other relevant parts of health services. To become a registered doctor, a student must successfully complete a five and a half year training course and a further eighteen months as a training house medical officer. Swedish medical research has a prominent international position in many fields. The training program for basic nursing lasts for three years.

**Compensation for patients**

If a patient suffers serious injury or illness in connection with medical care or treatment, or is exposed to the risk of injury or illness, the institution providing the care or treatment is obliged to report this to the National Board of Health and Welfare. Where faults or negligence are attributable to members of staff, the matter can be referred to the National Medical Disciplinary Board (Hälso- och sjukvårdens ansvarsnämnd), a government authority whose organization is somewhat similar to that of a court. A patient or a patient's relative can approach the Board if he or she considers that staff members of the health service have acted incorrectly. The Board decides on disciplinary measures and settles almost all patient complaints; they rarely reach the Swedish court system.

The Board does not deal with financial compensation for a patient—a patient insurance scheme covers such claims. Since 1997, every provider of health care has been legally obliged to provide, via insurance coverage, compensation for injuries that occur in the course of these services. A patient who has been injured, infected or has met with an accident in connection with an examination or treatment can be compensated, regardless of whether it is the responsibility of the medical services or not.

**Challenges**

Sweden has one of the oldest populations in the world, in which there are more people over eighty years of age per thousand than in any other EU country. The challenge is how to control health care costs while continuing to provide a high-class health care service.

## Conclusions about the health care systems in the countries considered

It is clear that there are basically two types of universal health care systems. Canada, England, Norway, Sweden, and Spain have mainly publicly funded systems, while those of Australia, France, Japan, and Germany use a combination of public and private funds. There are also varying degrees of control exerted by the government in each of these countries, in allowing private health insurance companies. In the case of Cuba, however, it is a completely publicly funded universal system.

No system of health care is perfect, and care is rationed, to an extent, in all countries.

While each country mentioned has its own unique problems to solve, it is also clear that the soaring cost of drugs and the increasing percentage of elderly in the population are problems common to all of them.

# Chapter IV

## The American Health Care System

The American colonies broke from Great Britain in 1776. The United States of America was born following the treaty of Paris in 1783. Initially only thirteen states participated in the birth of the nation. During the nineteenth and twentieth centuries, thirty-seven new states joined. Two of the most traumatic experiences in U.S. history were the Civil War (1861-65) and the Great Depression in the 1930s.

America is the most powerful country, and the richest country in the world. It was greatly responsible for the Allies winning both World War I and World War II, and is a founding member of both the United Nations (UN) and the North Atlantic Treaty Organization (NATO). It is a land of immigrants.

The American federal government, with the help of the fifty states, has the main responsibility for developing and implementing the health care programs of Medicaid, Medicare, and those for veterans, while private health insurance policies cover the rest of the population. In 2009, nearly 48 million people are uninsured and millions more are under-insured.

### General information

The United States of America has an area of 9,826,630 sq km, which includes the fifty states and the District of Columbia. The land area of the United States is slightly larger than China. It is the third largest country by size after Russia and Canada and by population after China and India.

## Other statistics

The population of the United States exceeded 303,824,640 in 2008. This estimate consisted of 81.7% white (including persons of Latin American descent), 12.9% black, 4.2% Asian, 1% Amerindian and Alaskan natives, and 0.2 % natives of Hawaii and other Pacific islands. Over the last two hundred years people from all parts of the world immigrated to the United States—making it the most powerful country and the largest economy in the world. It should be noted that there is no separate listing for Hispanics because the U.S Census Bureau considers Hispanic to mean a person of Latin American descent, including persons of Cuban, Mexican or Puerto Rican origin living in the U.S, who may be of any race or ethnic group (white, black, Asian etc).

There was a net migration of 2.92 migrants per thousand of population. The growth rate of the population was 0.88% in 2008. The median age of the population was 36.7 years, while the infant mortality rate was 6.3 deaths per thousand live births, and climbing. Average life expectancy was 78.14 years. For males, it was 75.29 years, and it was 81.13 years for females. The literacy rate was 97% for those over the age of fifteen.

The United States economy is the most capitalist and market oriented in the world. It has the largest and most technologically powerful economy, estimated at around \$14 trillion a year. The gross domestic product (GDP) was \$45,100 in purchasing power parity. U.S business firms enjoy considerably greater flexibility than those in Western European countries. The economic growth rate was 2.4% with an unemployment rate of 5.5% in 2007. The inflation rate was 2.5%. The poverty level was around 12%.

## Health care system

The U.S. health care system is neither a free market system, nor a universal one. It is a dysfunctional combination of both public and private funding. Hence, it is a restricted market system where consumers cannot register discontent about their insurance plans because it is difficult to switch them. Because of this difficulty, plans fail to provide quick resolution of claims, good information, or consistent policy, as customers are tied in to their current plans through their employers and because of the difficulty of switching plans.

The American health care system is a combination of jointly funded federal and state government entitlement programs, and private health insurance companies that insure most of the population. This includes the District of Columbia and U.S. territories. The government programs of Medicare and Medicaid are administered under the Health and Human Services department and state governments. Medicare is the federal health insurance program for people 65 and older, certain younger people with disabilities, people with end-stage renal disease (permanent kidney failure requiring dialysis or a transplant). Medicaid is a joint federal and state program that helps with the medical costs of people with low incomes and limited resources. Medicare programs vary from state to state, but most health care costs are covered if a person qualifies for both Medicare and Medicaid. There are also health care entitlement programs that vary from one state to another. For example, children under the age of eighteen may be covered for health care in one state, but this may not apply in another state.

The Department of Veterans Affairs (VA) is responsible for operating nationwide programs for health care services for veterans and their families. The VA is the second largest of the fifteen cabinet departments and is headed by the Secretary of Veterans Affairs. Armed forces personnel (present and past, including their families) are mainly entitled to health care services under the VA.

Apart from the federal and state health care programs of Medicare, Medicaid, and the VA, most people have private health insurance plans, through either their work place with federal or state governments or through their work with private companies. The self-employed have private health insurance plans. There are hundreds of health insurance companies providing all kinds of health insurance policies with varying degrees of deductibles and co-payments. With almost all health insurance policies, there is a varying degree of contributions possible from each employee and different co-payments for each kind of health service at the point of delivery. Health Maintenance Organizations (HMOs) are a popular form of health insurance. There are also Preferred Provider Organizations

(PPOs), which operate on a set fee basis. They offer more choice but cost more and cover only 80% of the charges. Most policies exceed $10,000 a year for a family of four. More than 47 million uninsured people are not eligible for any of the programs funded by federal and state governments.

Health care spending accounted for nearly 16% of America's GDP for the year 2006, in an economy of over $12 trillion. This means that health care spending amounted to nearly 2 trillion dollars, which is equal to spending $6,000 for each person per year, if we take the population of America as 300 million people. This makes U.S. health care spending per person nearly twice, on average, that of the rich countries of Europe, Japan, Australia and Canada. There was an increase in health care spending of over 6.5% in 2004, rising to nearly 16% by the end of 2005. It is expected to reach 20% of the GDP by 2013–14.

Figure 9 shows OECD data for pharmaceutical expenditure per capita, for major industrialized countries in 2006. During this time, health care spending in the U.S. was 15.3% of the GDP. American health care and pharmaceutical expenditures were higher than those of any other country in the world were, and they still are.

Figure 9

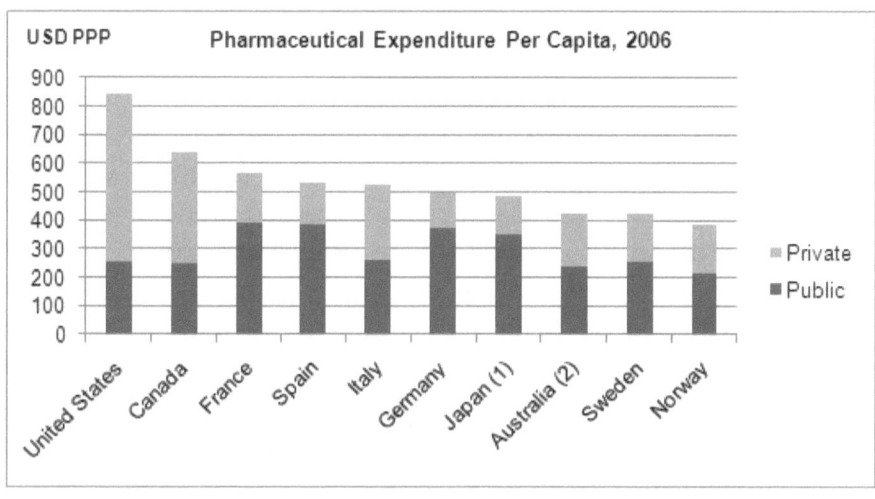

Source: *OECD Health Data 2008*, June 2008
(1) 2005 (2) 2005/06

## A little history

In the1900s, America lagged behind European countries in finding value in insuring against the costs of health care services. In 1901, the American Medical Association (AMA) became a powerful body and its membership of physicians increased to nearly 70,000 by 1910. This was half the number of physicians in the country at that time. Doctors were no longer obliged to provide free medical services to all the hospital patients. The American Association for Labor Legislation (AALL) and other progressive reformers argued for health insurance for all Americans but there was opposition from physicians and other interest groups. The entry of the U.S. into World War I in 1917 undermined the reform of health insurance.

After the end of war, the reformers again emphasized the cost of health care instead of wages lost to sickness but did not accomplish much in passing laws to provide health care for the American population. In the late 1920s, General Motors signed a contract with Metropolitan Life to insure its 180,000 workers for health care services.

In the 1930s, Congress passed the Social Security Act, which omitted health insurance. With the depression in the early part of the decade, there was emphasis on providing unemployment insurance and 'old age benefits' in the Social Security Act, rather than health insurance. The Blue Cross company began to offer private coverage for hospital care in dozens of states.

During World War II President Roosevelt's government passed wage and price control laws. In order to attract workers, companies began to offer health benefits that led to the present day employer-based health insurance plans. President Roosevelt asked Congress for an 'economic bill of rights,' including the right to adequate medical care. Later President Truman offered a national health program plan, which proposed a single system that would include all of American society. The American Medical Association and other interest groups denounced Truman's plan, so it never passed Congress.

Health care expenditure was 4.5% of the GDP in early 1950. A system of private health insurance developed for those who could afford it, and the federal responsibility for the sick and the poor was firmly established. Many legislative proposals were made with different approaches to solving the health insurance problem, but none succeeded. During the 1950s, the cost of health care in hospitals doubled. By the1960s, it became difficult for the elderly to afford health insurance despite there being over 700 companies selling health insurance policies. Major medical insurance companies endorsed high-cost medicine.

President Lyndon Johnson signed Medicare and Medicaid into law in July 1965. President Truman proposed such a program in 1945. The chances of passing legislation for compulsory health insurance for the whole population receded.

President Richard Nixon renamed prepaid group health care plans as Health Maintenance Organizations (HMOs), with legislation that provided federal endorsement, certification, and assistance. In the1970s, health care costs escalated rapidly due to rapidly rising inflation and the increasing cost of Medicare because of greater use of technology and better medications. President Nixon also proposed a national health insurance plan but both labor unions and liberals rejected it.

In the 1980s, companies began to integrate the hospital system, which was previously decentralized, and entered into many other health care related businesses. This was done to consolidate control. Under President Reagan, there was a general shift toward privatization of health care, and Medicare shifted to payment by diagnosis (DRG) instead of by treatment. There were growing complaints by health care insurance companies that the traditional fee-for-service method of payment to doctors was being exploited. Later the 'cap' on payments to doctors became more common.

In the early 1990s, health care costs rose at double the inflation rate. There was an expansion of managed care, which helped to moderate increases in these costs. President Clinton proposed federal universal health care reform legislation, which failed to pass in the U.S. Congress. Health care costs steadied for four years under the Clinton administration but have been rising sharply since then.

Since 2003, there has also been a sharp increase in advertisements of prescription drugs directed at the consumer.

Merck withdrew the drug Vioxx from advertising due to adverse effects on patients who were taking it. The FDA approved Vioxx in 1999. President Bush signed complicated legislation for prescription drugs for seniors in 2003.

President Roosevelt proposed legislation for universal health care insurance for the population nearly seventy years ago. Despite the efforts of several American Presidents to achieve a universal health care system, it has not been achieved, and over 47 million people remain uninsured and millions more are under-insured.

## Medicare, Medicaid, the VHA, and SCHIP

Medicare and Medicaid entitlement programs have evolved since their inception in 1965. These are both complex programs according to the Health and Human Services Department.

Medicare provides health insurance to nearly 40 million elderly and, in 1999, it cost the government $213 billion, or 12% of the federal budget, according to the Public Broadcasting System (PBS). The Medicare population is growing and it is expected to reach over 76 million people if Medicare is continued in the present form. It is already the third largest government program, and its spending as a percentage of the federal budget has doubled in just twenty years.

Many experts believe that America will need to find additional sources for funding Medicare in the future as the population of seniors rises. Some have suggested more taxes on products like tobacco and/ or greater contributions from America's wealthier seniors for further funding of Medicare.

Marcia Angell, MD, Editor-in-Chief of the *New England Journal of Medicine* said in an interview with PBS:

> In fact, the most successful part of the American health care system is Medicare. And Medicare, which is a single-payer, government financed health care system—what Canada has essentially is Medicare for everyone—but this is a government financed, single-payer system for

people over 65 and it's the most popular part of our health care system now.

*Medicare Part A* is the Medicare Hospital Insurance Trust Fund to which over 150 million employees make mandatory contributions. It finances inpatient hospital services, continued treatment, or rehabilitation at a nursing facility, and hospice care for the terminally ill, according to PBS. All eligible beneficiaries are automatically enrolled in Part A.

*Medicare Part B* is a medical insurance plan that helps pay for doctors' services, outpatient hospital care, and durable medical services that are not covered by Medicare Part A. Enrollment is voluntary under Part B.

*Medicare Prescription Drug Coverage (Part D)* is the prescription drug benefit for seniors that was signed into law by President George W. Bush as part of the Medicare Prescription Drug, Improvement, and Modernization Act of 2003. It went into effect in 2006, and serves as an addition to the existing Medicare programs.

*Medicare Advantage Plans* were introduced at the same time as Part D and offer more choice between health plans. Everyone who has Medicare Parts A and B is eligible (except those who have end-stage renal disease unless certain exceptions apply). Private health insurance companies offer Medicare Advantage policies that range in cost from no fee to over $100 a month for an individual. Plans can be for health services alone, or can include prescription drug coverage. Participants in these plans must still pay their Part B premium. They must also use the health card issued by the insurance company, instead of their Medicare card.

*Medigap Policies* are supplemental policies, sold by private insurance companies, to fill 'gaps' in the original Medicare Plan. There are twelve standardized plans labeled A through L that offer different levels of coverage across the states. After the January 1, 2006, implementation of Medicare Plan D, Medigap policies no longer offered drug coverage.

*Medicare-approved drug discount cards* were introduced in 2004 as an interim measure to help seniors save money on prescription drugs until Plan D was implemented. These cards offered different discounts for different drugs made by different companies, so that seniors had to choose the drug card that meshed best with their prescription medicine. They have been discontinued.

There are also Medicare plans that apply only regionally, or to people with special needs, as well as a limited number of new 'social managed-care plans' for the elderly. In general, Medicare does not cover long-term care.

Medicare has been evolving during the past decade. When it was signed into law in 1965, prescription drugs were not a major component of health care so there was no provision for a prescription drug benefit. Seniors had to pay for prescription drugs themselves. With advances in medical research resulting in more effective and more expensive drugs for particular illnesses, seniors began to spend as much as a third of their income on prescriptions. However, Medicare Parts A and B still did not cover drugs dispensed in an outpatient setting. Thus, the average senior began to spend more out of pocket for prescription drugs than for any other type of health care. Many seniors cannot afford the increasing cost of filling their prescriptions despite having supplemental insurance coverage. Some of them resort to taking less than their prescribed doses while others share drugs with their spouses—and some of them turn to crossing the border to Canada or Mexico to purchase their drugs, where the price is reasonable.

Details of the upcoming 2006 Medicare reforms resulting from the 2003 Medicare Prescription Drug, Improvement, and Modernization Act of 2003 were announced in 2005 by Tommy Thompson, former Secretary of Health and Human Resources. They included prescription drug coverage under Medicare Part D to save seniors money on prescription drugs, and new preventive benefits, including a 'Welcome to Medicare' physical exam for people when they first join, as well as screening to detect heart disease and diabetes early.

Before Congress approved the legislation in 2003, initial cost estimates of the prescription drug benefit were put at $400 billion over ten years. This estimate was adjusted to $534 billion two months later after it was signed into law, and then to $724 billion by early 2005. President Bush said that the new drug insurance "will save seniors from a lot of worry." Critics of the bill said that the worries had just begun for Medicare's 40 million older and disabled people.

Many seniors and disabled people relied on supplemental insurance under Medigap policies to pay the cost of their prescription drugs before these policy rules were changed. Some Medicaid beneficiaries feared severe restrictions would be placed on their drug coverage.

The government stated that the monthly premium for the drug plan would be a national average of $35 per month in 2006, but the cost of the premium could differ from one region of the country to the next. There is nothing in the law that precludes private insurance companies from offering more generous or costly plans.

When Plan D first came out, after paying for the first $250 in prescriptions, seniors were responsible for 25 % of the next $2,000 in drug costs. The government paid nothing for drug costs from $2,250 to $5,100. Above that, 'catastrophic coverage' kicked in, and the government paid all but 5% of the remaining prescription costs for the year. Although Medicare regulates the maximum rates for these categories, there is an enormous variety of insurance plans offering Plan D coverage, and premiums and deductibles vary greatly. By 2007, the deductible limit had already risen by 6%, and the catastrophic limit, by 11%.

The new prescription drug law runs more than 700 pages and the choices for seniors are daunting. There are 60 plans to choose from in San Diego County, 52 plans in Virginia and 24 plans in Alaska—according to a PBS report on November 11, 2005. All these plans have different premiums, co-payments, and deductibles. The drug benefit plans baffle many seniors and they struggle to understand their options.

Unfortunately, the law excludes the federal government from bargaining to buy drugs in bulk from pharmaceutical companies, which would reduce prices—yet the government negotiates the bulk buying of drugs under the Department of Veterans Affairs.

Information about the number of other complicated Medicare Plans and the cost of drugs is available at www.medicare.gov or by calling 1-800-MEDICARE.

*Medicaid* is a publicly funded insurance program which, according to a report on PBS, covers over 41 million people in America. It is Title XIX of the Social Security Act, which is a federal/state entitlement program that pays for medical assistance for certain individuals and families with low incomes and resources. This program became law in 1965 as a cooperative venture that is jointly funded by Federal and State governments (including the District of Columbia and the territories) in order to assist states in furnishing medical assistance to eligible needy people. Medicaid is the largest source of funding for medical and health-related services for the poor in the United States.

Federal statutes, regulations, and policies, established broad national guidelines under which each state does the following

- Establishes its own eligibility standards

- Determines the type, amount, duration, and scope of services

- Sets the rate of payment for services

- Administers its own programs

The Medicaid policies for eligibility, services, and payment are complex and can vary between states. A person eligible for Medicaid in one state may not be eligible in another state, and the scope and duration of services provided also varies from state to state. In addition, state legislatures can also change Medicaid eligibility, services, and reimbursements at any time.

Under the provisions of the Federal statutes, Medicaid does not provide health care services even for very poor persons unless they fall into one of the groups that are defined and designated. States have broad discretion in determining which groups their Medicaid programs will cover and the financial criteria for eligibility. In addition, there are 'State-only' programs to provide medical assistance for specific low income categories that do not qualify for Medicaid. Federal matching funds are provided to states according to criteria set by federal eligibility regulations. The criteria of eligibility, duration of medical services and reimbursements can change from time to time—and these criteria are constantly evolving.

Medicaid operates as a vender payment program and payments are made directly to the providers of health care. Medicaid sets the reimbursement level of payment to providers that participate in its programs. Each state has broad discretion in determining (within federally imposed upper limits and specific restrictions) the reimbursement methodology and the resulting rate of services, with three exceptions:

- For institutional services, payment may not exceed amounts that would be paid under Medicare payment rates

- For disproportionate share hospitals (DSHs)

- For hospital care

States may impose nominal deductibles, co-insurance, or co-payments, on some of the Medicaid recipients' services. Family planning and emergency services are exempt for such co-payments. Certain Medicaid recipients are excluded from cost sharing. This group is pregnant women, children under the age of eighteen, hospital, or nursing home patients who are expected to contribute most of their income to institutional care, and categorically needy HMO enrollee

The federal government matches in payment whatever the individual state decides to provide in health care services, within the law, for its eligible recipients. The amount of total federal outlays for Medicaid has no set limit. With skyrocketing costs in the Medicaid program, Congress is looking into ways to cut costs for recipients of Medicaid services.

Medicaid services are very complex. Detailed information about co-payments, eligibility, and other criterion can be obtained by visiting either www.cms.hhs.gov/publications/overview-medicare-medicaid/ or by visiting each state's related website.

*The Veterans Health Administration (VHA)* is a part of the Department of Veterans Affairs (VA), established on March 15, 1989, to succeed the Veterans Affairs Administration. The VA is responsible for providing federal benefits to eligible veterans and their families.

Headed by the Secretary of Veterans Affairs, it is the second largest of the fifteen cabinet departments, operating nationwide programs for health care, financial assistance, and burial benefits.

There are nearly 25 million veterans currently alive, and according to the VA, approximately 63 million people (including family members and survivors of veterans) are potentially eligible for VHA benefits. In the VA's fiscal year 2004 spending, $29.1 billion was marked for health care services for eligible veterans and their families. The health care budget was $37.3 billion in 2007, and increased to $47.2 billion in 2009—an increase of nearly 60% since 2004. All working personnel in uniform and their families get free health care. The rest of the veterans have varying degrees of eligibility for health care under the VHA.

Medical care is the most visible part of VA benefits. The number of veteran patients treated was over 5 million in the year 2004 as illustrated in figure10.

Figure 10

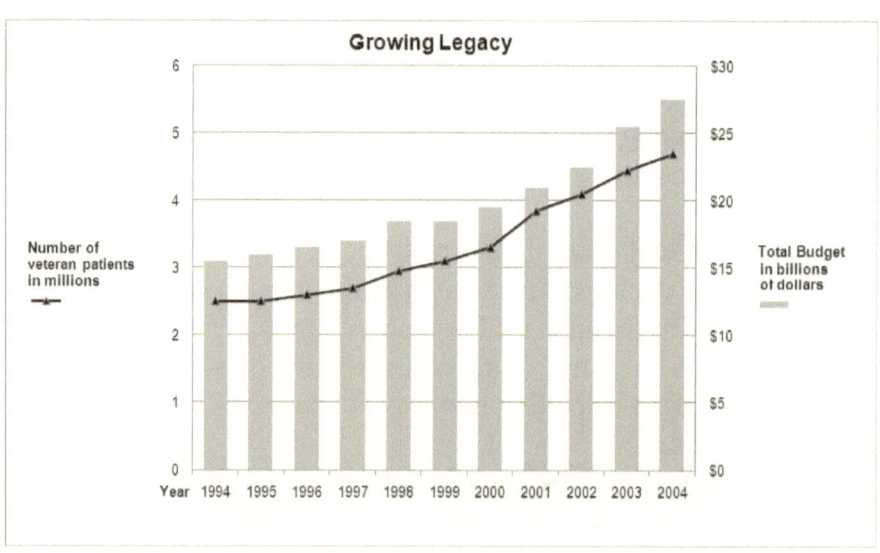

Source: Department of Veterans Affairs

The veteran's health care system had 157 medical centers, with at least one in each state, Puerto Rica and the District of Columbia in 2004. The VA also operates more than 1,300 other sites for medical care, including 862 ambulatory care and community-based outpatient clinics, 134 nursing homes, 42 residential rehabilitation treatment programs, 207 Veterans centers, and 88 comprehensive home-care programs, according to the department. In general, VA health care facilities provide a broad spectrum of medical, surgical, and rehabilitative care.

There were over 5 million veterans receiving VA health care during this time. Nearly 78% of all disabled and low-income veterans had enrolled with the VA and over 65% of these were treated. VA inpatient facilities treated 587,000 patients and outpatient clinics registered nearly 54 million visits in 2004. The VA also provides health care and benefits to more than 100,000 homeless veterans each year.

The VA manages the largest medical education and health professions training program in the U.S. It is affiliated with 107 medical schools, 55 dental schools and more than 1,200 other schools across the U.S. It is estimated that more than half of the physicians practicing in America had some of their professional education in the VA health care system.

The VA is actively involved in research in health care related fields. In 2005, the estimated funding for research was nearly $800 million. Further funding from non-VA sources such as the National Institutes of Health, other government agencies and pharmaceutical companies, contributed another $800 million to VA research. More than a decade ago, Republicans rejected President Clinton's health care reform. Nevertheless, although Clinton lost, he established a foothold for his ideas in the Veterans Health Administration (VHA). His administration brought in managers who decentralized the structure of the old VA system, and invested in improving health care for veterans, in a way similar to primary-care clinic models developed in Britain.

Legislators are still investing billions of dollars per year in the veterans' health care system. Annual spending on the VHA has grown by 58% after inflation. Part of this explosive growth in spending on health care has been due to extensive involvement of America's armed forces in Afghanistan and Iraq.

Despite the steep rise in its annual budget and shortcomings in the VHA's handling of disability claims, the department is at the forefront of instituting new information technology for medical records and negotiating lower prices for drugs for each veteran.

The persistent lobbying by veterans, as well as the wars in Afghanistan and Iraq, have resulted in Congress voting for substantial budget increases for the VA and increasingly opening the health care system to more veterans. In wartime, the department has become too much of a patriotic symbol, hence it is almost unthinkable not to increase its budget annually. President Bush has boasted that in his first four years in office, he increased VA spending by twice as much as the Clinton administration had in eight years.

Mr. Kenneth Kizer, Mr. Clinton's undersecretary for VA health care from 1994–99 stated, "In some ways, the VA has become the victim of its own success. More and more people want to use it." There has been steady growth in the number of patients who have become eligible enrollees, as they have no public or private health insurance. More Vietnam War veterans are turning to the VHA as they age and are using it as a backup for shortfalls in any other health insurance coverage they do have.

If the VA's sophisticated electronic patient record system became standard in the rest of the health care industry it would lead to some cost reduction in medical care. The VA also negotiates and then bulk buys drugs from pharmaceutical companies, which cuts the cost of prescription drugs for patients. It is amazing that the same principle was not applied in the new prescription drug law for seniors in January 2006.

Medicare, Medicaid, and the VHA are all complex, publicly funded programs, run jointly by federal and state administrations under statutes passed by Congress. The legislators set the budget appropriations; however, over 40% of total health care spending in America is due to the entitlement programs that have evolved under this system over the years. The success of these entitlement programs has created problems, as well as large bureaucracies. One of the major issues is the question of who is actually eligible for each program. The criterion for eligibility can be quite complex— leading to bureaucracy. On top of this is the fact that each state has its own additional and varied entitlement programs, leading to even further bureaucracy! Several friends of mine, who are doctors and who work in administering these programs, have complained that it is hard to grasp all the state and federal regulations and even tougher to implement them.

*The State Children's Health Insurance Program (SCHIP)* is a relatively new, still evolving, federally funded health insurance program created by the Balanced Budget Act of 1997 signed by President Clinton. It is Title XXI of the Social Security Act, and was initially enacted for a ten-year period. State administered SCHIP programs provide coverage to low income children who are not eligible for Medicaid. Unlike Medicaid, federal funds that are allocated to participating states are capped.

Australia, Germany, Japan, and all other rich industrialized nations with universal health care follow the social-insurance model. Medicare, Medicaid, VHA programs, and SCHIP, are also based on the social-insurance model. People who are registered with such programs feel consistently happier with virtually every aspect of their insurance coverage than people with private insurance do. It is not that people registered with entitlement programs get better health care than the ones insured privately, but they consider that the security of entitlement programs insulates them against the financial shock of serious illness.

**Health Insurance and HMOs**

The federal and state governments "provide coverage to a large number of Americans both as an employer (39.2 million for federal, state and local government employees, including the military) and through public insurance programs such as Medicare (39 million) and Medicaid (41 million)," according to a report on PBS. These figures must have increased, as well, since the last count was made. Over 120 million people get primary health insurance from their employers. There are over 47 million people who are uninsured and the number is increasing, and still millions more who are under-insured. Most of these people have separate dental insurance.

The cost of health insurance has been rising dramatically and far surpassing the general rate of inflation for the last fifteen years. PBS also reported that the average amount an employee had to contribute for family coverage jumped from $935 to $1,778 from 1989 to 1996. In 1990, American companies spent $177 billion on health care benefits for employees and their dependents—that number rose to $252 billion by 1996,—which was more than double the rate of inflation. The cost of employee and company contributions for health care has further exploded since then, leading many companies, including General Motors (GM), to renegotiate employee contracts with respect to cutting the cost of health care insurance by increasing contributions from employees, and reducing health care benefits for their retirees.

In general, employees, consumers and taxpayers pay for the rising costs of health insurance. Companies pass along a portion of rising premiums to their workforces in the form of lower wage increases. Government entitled health programs cost 47% of the health care tab in the U.S. Spending on health care makes up over 20% of the federal budget and is on the rise, and this does not include spending on health care in each state. If a person paid $5,000 in federal taxes, around $1,000 went to health care programs. (Source: http//ww.nchc.org)

*Health Maintenance Organizations (HMOs)* are a type of managed plan wherein a group of doctors, hospitals, and other health care providers agree to provide health care to beneficiaries for a set amount of money every month. Patients get their care only from the providers in the plan. Medicare patients can enroll their benefits in an HMO plan.

Initially, HMOs developed on the pattern of what was known as a prepaid group practice – organizations like Kaiser Permanente or Group Health Cooperative provided health care. These organizations were both the providers and the insurers. In the 1990s, the two roles tended to split with the advancement of the managed care movement. Hence, HMO as a term is increasingly being used as the insurance part and not for the delivery of health care. The HMO, as insurer, had a network of health care providers—a network of doctors and a network of hospitals—but did not feel responsible for providing health care and became more of a contractor of a network. Doctors have tried to get together into networks of various kinds but a lot of them have not worked well. Hospitals have also been developing their own health care systems and a number of those have not been working well either, according to Rosemary Stevens, PhD, Professor of History & Sociology of Science, University of Pennsylvania.

Some seniors have drug coverage under Medicare HMOs, which along with other forms of managed care; have been able to negotiate lower prices for prescription drugs from the pharmaceutical companies, but people paying for their medications as individuals cannot take advantage of these discounted rates. Therefore, the people who do not have drug coverage are less likely to fill prescriptions that their doctors give them, and are less likely to take medication that can improve their health and prevent the more serious effects of chronic diseases from developing.

There are hundreds of insurance companies providing health insurance plans to large and medium size companies, small businesses, and the self-employed. Each state may have up to 100 types of these plans, which vary in terms of the cost of the plan, deductibles, and co-payments. It is left up to consumers to decide which plan is suitable for them and their families. The plans, written by lawyers, are complex so there is a certain amount of ambiguity in the language used.

Almost all large and medium sized companies offer health insurance plans to their permanent employees. They negotiate these plans with the insurance industry. Companies make a major contribution towards their employees' health insurance plans, but employees contribute as well. Companies may not necessarily offer coverage to all their employees. Many do not offer health care to their part-time workers. Employees lose their coverage when they leave the company either voluntarily, or upon dismissal from their position.

Wal-Mart Inc., the largest retailer in the world, has eighteen different types of health care policies. The company employs over 1.2 million workers worldwide, but does not cover all their employees for health benefits. In general, part-time workers and their families do not get any coverage. CNN reported on October 29, 2005, that over 600,000 Wal-Mart workers and their families had no health care benefits.

**Doctors, hospitals and clinics**

People with insurance go to their doctors for medical problems they may be facing. Insured people can make an appointment to go to their doctor's office for an examination at any time. They also have a chance to choose their own doctor or practice. More and more doctors have joined to form multi-doctor practices. They are doing this in order to afford in-house equipment for performing simple tests, such as on blood and urine, on their patients. By having in-house equipment, practices can save both time and money—otherwise, they would have to send samples of blood from their patients to specialized labs for results. After examining a patient, the practice may either give him or her a suitable medication, or refer the patient to a specialist or a relevant hospital. Some doctors and practices are refusing to take any more Medicare or Medicaid patients.

America has some of the finest hospitals in the world, contributing to high quality research and to the education of quality and competent doctors. Despite having high caliber personnel in the delivery of health care, nearly 100,000 patients die per year because of mistakes made by the staff working in hospitals. These mistakes are mostly in the form of dispensing the wrong dose of medicine, or the wrong medicine being given to a patient, infection through intravenous feeding tubes, forgetting to cleanse hands or instruments before examining patients, assigning wrong labels to patients, or some other form of negligence due to over work or tiredness.

Hospitals cannot refuse treatment to anybody in their emergency rooms, even if the patient has no health insurance. It is forbidden by law to deny treatment or medication to anybody visiting hospital emergency rooms. The hospital staff must try to stabilize the person's condition at least. Billing is done according to the status of each patient, whether insured or not, which leads to many oddities. The cost and system of billing is complex. The cost of a similar procedure, surgery, or other form of treatment varies between patients according to their insurance plans and to whether or not they are uninsured. The staff in the emergency room decides which patients should have priority in their treatment after an initial examination.

Most poor, low income or uninsured patients can also use the services of health care clinics, where dental service is also available. They either can walk into a clinic or can make an appropriate appointment to see a doctor. The patient pays to see the doctor according to a sliding scale of ability to pay, which is decided by a staff member of the clinic. An uninsured patient may have to wait for a longer time to see a doctor at the clinic than one who is insured, and is registered either with a doctor or with the practice. Patients can also buy prescription drugs at the clinic pharmacies at a lower, subsidized price.

**Faith-based and private institutions**

There are faith-based organizations that provide health care to needy and homeless people. There are also private foundations, including hospitals that operate on patients who cannot afford to pay the cost. Faith-based and private institutions raise money privately, either through private donors or through general fund-raising. There are also non-profit hospitals, including county hospitals, for the medical care of patients.

**Challenges**

America is facing serious challenges, both in keeping the ever rising cost of health care down, and in how to include un-insured people within the health care system. There are also serious problems and issues with government-funded programs, insurance and drug companies, lobbyists, mal-practice health insurance and legal costs, problems of bureaucracy, and with electronic data kept for each patient. Chapter 5 highlights and discusses these problems and issues.

# Chapter V

# Problems and Issues Related to the American Health Care System

The rising cost of health care is the biggest challenge among American politicians, business executives, workers, and retirees. The reform of the health care system is even more important and urgent than that of the Social Security system. On October 19, 2005, U.S. Democratic Representative John Dingell (Michigan), who has served fifty years in the House of Representatives, stated on this matter on the Charlie Rose program. He said, "The reform of health care is the most important domestic topic."

There is an inclination in parts of the media and amongst many politicians in the United States to blame some external forces beyond control whenever there is trouble with a certain section of the American economy. To clarify this sentence further:

- For many years, people blamed the leading Detroit automakers grief on unfair trade and corporate policies practiced by Japan, instead of on the automakers not adjusting to improve the quality and performance of their autos—blame the politicians and Japan.

- With the trade deficit exceeding $200 billion yearly with China, many Americans accept that low-cost labor in China has been the cause of the structural decline in U.S. manufacturing employment. The real culprits have been the insatiable appetite of American consumers for cheap goods produced in China, the decline of productivity in U.S. manufacturing, and the growth of the service industry in the U.S—blame the politicians and China.

- There has been a decline of jobs in the IT sector in America. Outsourcing of many of these jobs to India is common. The U.S. produces about 75,000 engineers and scientists a year while India produces over 350,000 a year. In this age of economic globalization, companies move jobs where it is the most cost effective—blame the politicians and India.

- There has been a steady rise of energy costs in the U.S. in the last few years. America has nearly 5% of the world population yet it absorbs about 25% of the world's energy resources. The cost of gasoline in the U.S. went up to over $4 per gallon in 2008. This is nearly half the cost in other rich countries in the world. It is easy to find fault with greedy global oil companies and Arab countries (the main producers of oil are Saudi Arabia, Kuwait, Iran, Iraq, Brunei, and other gulf states) but not American consumers—blame the oil companies and Arab countries.

- There is air pollution in Los Angles and global warming? It has been due do to coal-belching China or the Santa Ana winds, not the thousands of drivers clogging the freeways of Southern California—blame the politicians and other countries.

- Finally, there is the problem of illegal immigrants mainly from Mexico, who provide low cost labor working in the farming, hospitality, food processing, service, and construction industries. They are also very much a part of the domestic help industry; cleaning houses, tending gardens and acting as nannies and cooks for the middle to rich classes in America—blame the politicians and Mexico.

*There is one problem with these statements; Americans can blame neither China, nor India, nor Mexico, nor any other nation, for America's soaring cost of health care. America can not export a substantial part of the health care industry to other countries in order to make money because the health care system and its functioning are neither cost effective nor do they provide universal health care for residents of the United States.*

The expenditure on health care exceeded 15% of the GDP in 2006. Although the rate of increase in health costs has slowed to between 7–8% per annum in the last few years from double-digit inflation, it is still likely to remain more than double the rate of inflation in the coming years. Health care costs in America will reach 20% of the GDP by the year 2015, which is unsustainable. The GDP of health care in America would be the fifth largest economy in the world—amounting to well over 2 trillion dollars.

Figure 11 shows health care expenditure as a percentage of GDP for selected countries, which includes both public and private funding.

Figure 11

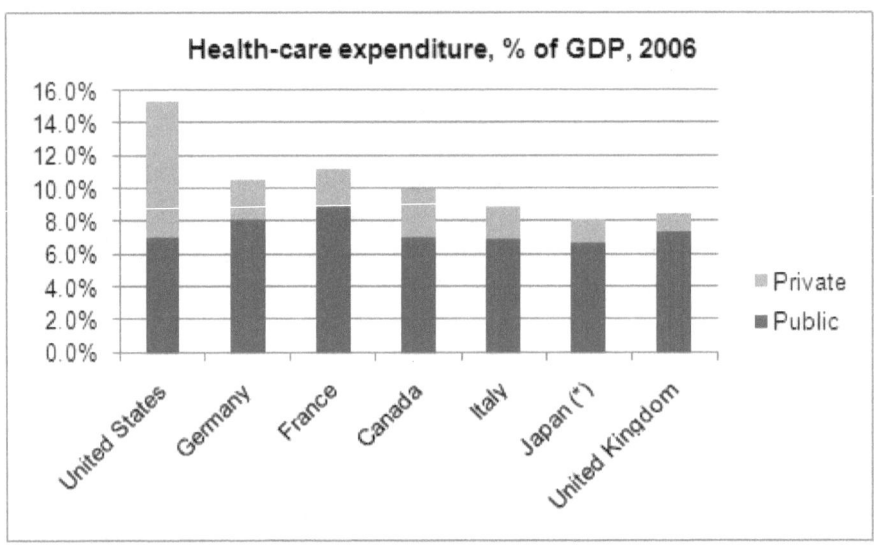

Source: OECD Health Data 2008, June 2008 * Japan data from 2005

It shows that U.S. government spending on health care—mainly Medicare, Medicaid and the VA—amounts to 7.2% of the GDP, while 55% of the health care bill is paid by individuals and companies. The public funded entitlement programs will exceed more than 50% of health care costs before the year 2013.

The economists in the Organization for Economic Cooperation and Development (OECD), a think-tank in Paris funded by thirty economically developed countries from Australia to the United States, are waving a red flag because of the alarming growth of health care spending in all the countries. Specifically in the U.S., OECD expects that public health care spending will reach 10–13% of its GDP by the year 2050. The biggest drivers of health care spending are the effect of rising incomes, the cost of medical technology, and the ever-increasing cost of prescription drugs in America. With the baby-boomers aging, the cost of health care will increase further. The OECD says, "A less commonly recognized driver is the cost of long-term care for disabled or elderly people who cannot eat, bathe, or dress themselves as families are less likely to provide this care."

According to an article by Sarah Skidmore that appeared in the *San Diego Union-Tribune*, older Americans are putting off retirement or returning to the work force to collect benefits and offset increases in health care costs. The average out-of-pocket health care spending for a married couple (at least one spouse is sixty-five or older) will be around 24% of their average after-tax income in 2010 as compared to 16% in 2000, according to data gathered by the Center for Retirement Research.

U.S. health care spending has increased from 6.5% of the GDP in 1970 to nearly 16% in 2005 according to the Kaiser Family Foundation—yet nearly 46 million people have no health insurance. If the U.S. health care system were a separate country it would be one of the ten largest economies in the world, producing growth rates that other rich nations would envy. The following table compares categories of the U.S. spending as a percentage of GDP.

Figure 12

| Year | Education | Defense | Health Care |
|------|-----------|---------|-------------|
| 1960 | 6% | 6% | 6% |
| 2005 | 6% | 4% | 16% |

In 1960, health care spending was equal to spending on education and equal to spending on defense, but by 2005 health care spending became equal to the sum of spending on education, defense, and the budgets of several other departments. Are Americans getting their money's worth? The answer is no. International expert George Schieber observed that "In comparison with other major industrial countries, health care in the United States costs more per person and per unit of service, is less accessible to a larger portion of its citizens, is provided at a more intensive level and offers comparatively poor gross outcomes." His comment reflects the opinion of most experts who study health care systems.

## The effect of rising health care costs

Major employers are under pressure to cut costs in order to compete in a global market but at the same time, they are facing ever-increasing costs of health care for their employees and retirees. Health care benefits promised to employees are becoming a crippling burden for a growing number of firms in America. More and more small businesses cannot even afford to provide health insurance for their staff. The cost of health insurance is shifting from employers to employees and is accelerating while access to health care has become more difficult.

General Motors (GM), the world's largest carmaker, announced in June 2005 that by 2008 there would be 25,000 job cuts out of a workforce of 118,000 in the United States. It costs on average an extra $1500 per GM car produced in the U.S. (in contrast to cars produced in other rich countries) due to health care insurance. This figure increases to $2500 per car if one includes benefits like pensions. The company has promised health care to over 1.2 million retirees and their dependents. GM reported after the market closed on March 16, 2006, that it had lost $10.6 billion in 2005 compared to its preliminary report of a loss of $8.6 billion.

Delphi, the biggest maker of car parts, was spun off in 1999 from GM and filed for Chapter11 bankruptcy protection; a dire consequence in part, of meeting health care obligations for its current employees and retirees. Delphi's future health care obligations alone are under-funded to a tune of over $5 billion. The bankruptcy of Delphi will also affect General Motors, according to the *Economist* of October 13, 2005, as GM's potential liability to Delphi ranges from $1.5 billion to $11 billion. GM relies heavily on Delphi for parts and says it could be contractually liable for up to $11 billion in benefits, including health care costs, to Delphi workers in the event of bankruptcy by the car part supplier.

GM extracted concessions from the United Auto Workers (UAW) wherein both its hourly workers and retirees pay more for their health care. According to a *Wall Street Journal* report of October 14, 2005, GM expected to save $1 billion a year in health costs, which could slash $20 billion from GM's health care obligations over time. Ford Motor Co. and DaimlerChrysler received similar concessions from the UAW. DaimlerChrysler reported on March 15, 2006, that it is increasing the cost of health care coverage for salaried employees and retirees under a plan that will leave top executives paying most or all of the cost of their medical insurance. What is unfortunate for General Motors is the same for much of corporate America.

GM's problems at its core North American auto operations have been building for many years. Since 2004, it has run up $72 billion in net losses. Ever-increasing health care costs for the labor force and retirees, and their dependents, have also contributed to these losses. Bailout funds poured into GM since December 2008 total over $17 billion. The corporation filed for bankruptcy in 2009 for restructuring purposes in order to survive and become profitable again. Toyota surged past GM in worldwide vehicle sales in 2008, thus becoming number one in unit sales.

Most of the major airlines, including Delta, US Air, Northwest, and United Airlines were either in Chapter11 bankruptcy or losing billions of dollars by the end of 2005 because of increasing costs, especially due to health care. Without a major reform in the health care system, United States companies and public sector employees will face a severe crisis within the next ten years.

Wal-Mart Stores Inc. is the largest retailer in the world, employing over 1.3 million people at the end of 2005 in the United States. At the beginning of 2006, less than 47% of Wal-Mart employees had health insurance according to the Henry J. Kaiser Family Foundation, a health care research group. There has been severe criticism of Wal-Mart over lack of health care coverage for its employees especially part-time workers. Wal-Mart's response was to offer a low-cost plan for employees who have worked for the company for at least six months. As reported in the *Wall Street Journal* on December 3–4, 2005, "The low-cost plan offers average monthly premiums of $23 for individuals, $37 for a single parent and $65 for a family—figures that Wal-Mart says are at least 40% lower than those in its other plans. However, as a trade-off, an annual deductible of $1,000 kicks in after three doctor visits per enrollee per year, and the plan has a $25,000 cap per enrollee in the first year of coverage. Union-backed groups have criticized the plan's deductibles and first-year cap as prohibitive for low-wage workers with health care needs." Despite the offer of a low-cost health care plan, only 49% of the work force of the largest retailer in the world had coverage for health care at the beginning of 2006. The majority of employees at the retailer earn barely more than the minimum wage of around $7 per hour.

AT&T, IBM, and other major companies are passing on increasing health care insurance costs to their employees, who also have to pay higher deductibles as health care costs rise. According to Starbucks Chairman Howard Schultz, the company spent more on health insurance for its employees in 2005 than on raw materials needed to brew its coffee due to double-digit increases in insurance costs each of the previous four years. Furthermore, he added, "It is completely non-sustainable." Considered one of the best service companies in providing health insurance to its employees, most of whom are under the age of thirty; Starbucks provides coverage for all who work at least twenty hours a week. We can only imagine what is happening in other major service companies.

The examples above are taken from one of the largest manufacturing employers, GM, and the largest retail employer, Wal-Mart, in order to illustrate the dilemma such companies face when insuring their employees with the health care plans in existence.

Most municipal governments in California and across the country are recognizing the problem of how to calculate, and then pay, the health care costs of their retirees, as most city governments are under-funded. Very few cities have set aside money for their future retiree health care obligations.

Jay Roeder, who worked for the San Diego pension system for thirteen years until the end of 2005, called retiree health benefits "the 800-pound gorilla" and "the number one financial issue for many entities in California right now" according to a *San Diego Union-Tribune* article of March 15, 2006.

*The availability and affordability of health care is the number one concern of the American population, according to a Gallup poll conducted March 13–16, 2006.*

According to the poll, out of a thousand Americans, 68% were worried about health care as the leading issue, with 51% placing concerns about Social Security second. Availability of energy came in third place with 48% of the respondents. The war in Iraq and the fight against terrorism has dominated the national dialogue and news coverage in recent years, yet they did not make Gallup's list of the top twelve concerns.

According to Tommy Thomson, ex-secretary of Health and Human Services (HHS), the number of un-insured will reach 54 million by the year 2010, and health insurance coverage by small businesses will decline from 74% in 2005 to 60% by 2015.

The key points that emerge from the rising cost of health care and its affordability and accessibility are:

- Over 47 million people are un-insured and millions are under-insured.

- The cost of health care is rising at least twice as fast as the rate of economic growth.

- Major companies and municipal governments are passing more of the cost of health care to their employees. Most of the companies and local governments will not be able to meet their obligations of health care to retirees.

- Many of the small businesses, especially in the service sector, do not even provide health insurance to their employees.

- Most of the companies and city governments have not set aside enough money to meet health care obligations to retired employees.

- More and more companies will shift their manufacturing to other countries because they will not be able to sustain health care costs for their employees in the U.S.

- There is a steady rise in bankruptcies amongst individuals as well as companies due to the cost of health care. There were over a million bankruptcies filed by individuals in 2005 who could not afford to pay their health care costs.

- The cost of prescription drugs is rising even faster than the general rise in health care costs.

- The rising cost of health care is unsustainable and it will lead to crisis in the not too distant future in the U.S.

What has brought about this situation, and why is the cost of health care rising so fast? Following is an examination of some of the problems and issues that contribute to the ever-increasing cost.

## Bureaucracy and paperwork

There has been a quantum leap in the amount of paperwork required to carry out the daily tasks of health care in the last twenty years. The increase is over 1,500%, a mind-boggling number. Charts presented by the Bureau of Labor Statistics confirm these figures. The growth in paperwork has lead to a vast expansion in the number of people required to administer the health care system. The following graph shows the comparative growth of physicians and administrators from 1970 to 1998.

Figure 13

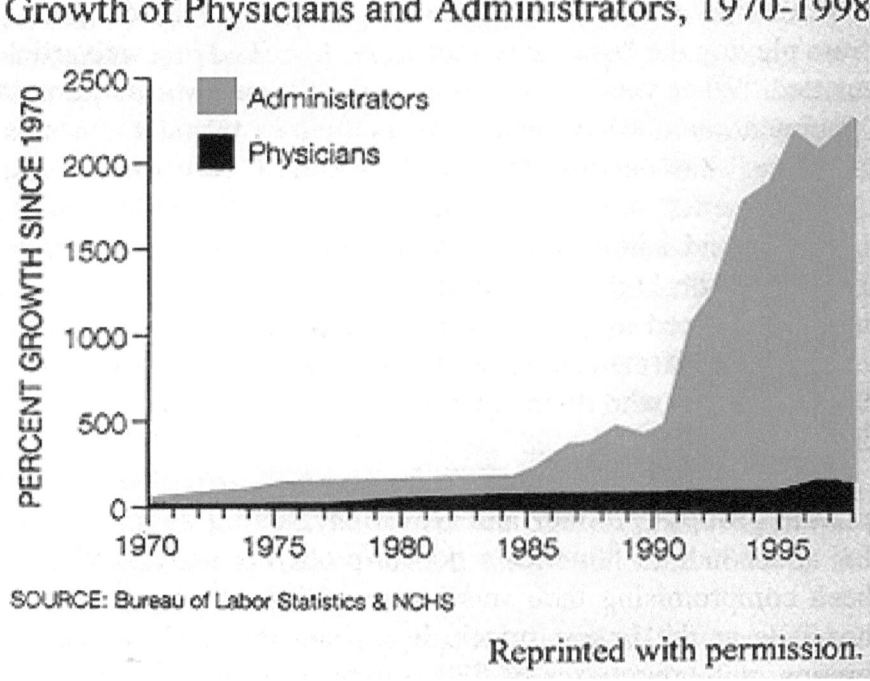

Source: Printed from *The Brave New World of Health Care* by former governor
of Colorado. Richard D. Lamm

There are the three major reasons for the enormous increase
in administrative costs:

1.  There is a great deal of fragmentation of private insurance.
    Over one 1,500 health insurers handle the private insurance
    market. All insurance companies have unique health policies
    with different deductibles. Then there are policies that cover
    only prescription drugs for seniors. In the state of California
    alone, there are nearly 150 combinations of drug insurance
    policies, each with different deductible amounts.

2.      There is compartmentalization of the delivery of health care in the United States. In his book, *The Brave New World of Health Care*, former governor of Colorado Richard Lamm writes:

> No health care system in the world even approaches the U.S. health care system for balkanization of delivery of health care. The federal government runs Medicare, while Medicaid is run by the states, though the federal government pays approximately 50 percent of Medicaid. We have separate health care programs for veterans (Why do we have/need 174 veteran's hospitals?), and separate programs for dependents of our military. Fifteen hundred health insurers handle the private insurance market. This balkanization prevents any payer from getting enough leverage on the system to gain efficiencies and massive amounts of extra overhead are engendered.
>
> The excesses of the American health care system, as enumerated above (and by no means are all listed), are a national tragedy.

He went on to write further, "At some point, historians are going to look back at America and wonder how any society could be as reckless with their limited resources."

3.      There are a great deal of problems related to eligibility for various entitlement programs and insurance plans. Universal coverage and health insurance system that enrolled everyone automatically would readily solve most of the problems with eligibility.

The current U.S. health care system is organizationally chaotic. According to some estimates, the United States spends over 30% of its health care dollars on bureaucracy, while other rich nations spend around 10%. Each health care transaction in the U.S. generates, on average, fifteen pieces of paper. This paperwork is generated as doctors, hospitals and administrative staff sort out which of the over 1,500 insurance companies, in 50 states, and which federal and state agencies they have to bill, for a patient's services. The demands of managed-care organizations consume more and more time from health care providers and lead to even more paperwork.

The United States health care system spends bundles of money on drug advertising, expenses of sales representatives, underwriting costs, claims adjusters, claims administration, and staff bureaucracy—the rich countries of Europe, as well as Japan, Australia, and Canada, avoid these expenses a great extent.

A study in 2002 by Donald Light showed that 2,277 people in the Seattle health insurance market were covered by 755 different health insurance policies and 189 different health care plans. According to Richard Lamm, "An NBC special on health care showed a 300-bed hospital in Bellingham, Washington, which had 42 billing clerks. A few miles away in Vancouver, British Columbia, a 300-bed hospital had 1 billing clerk."

The implementation of information technology processes to accumulate and update medical data about patients electronically will play a major role in cutting costs and making health care in any system more efficient and cost effective. Thus, it is imperative to invest funds in the health-data systems needed to improve the organization and delivery of health care. There is no reason why a newborn cannot have an electronic chip implanted under the skin for keeping health records, which health officials could access throughout his or her life.

## Fragmentation and eligibility inefficiencies in entitlement programs

There are three major problems with the entitlement programs funded and run either by the federal government, the states, or by a combination of both. All lead to massive paperwork and the net effect is inefficient delivery of health care. They are:

- The fragmentation of insurance coverage

- The eligibility factor

- The prevention of fraud

All these problems have created paperwork and controls, greatly increasing administrative costs and hassles. The diverse nature of entitlement programs with an 'eligibility factor' further adds to administrative costs. Universal health care coverage would greatly reduce administrative costs, as would a health insurance system that enrolled everyone automatically.

There is too much fragmentation of insurance company health care policies covering individuals, businesses, and state and federal employees. According to some estimates, there are over one 1,500 insurance companies all over the United States. These companies offer complicated lists of plans, with varying charges for premiums, deductibles, and co-payments. Only the attorneys who write them can understand some of the language in these plans. This fragmentation of insurance coverage for citizens leads to disputes and enormous amounts of paperwork.

Robert H. LeBow, M.D[5], writes in his book, *Health Care Meltdown: Confronting the Myths and Fixing our Failing System*:

---

[5]    *Robert LeBow, MD, MPH, was the Medical Director of a community health center in Idaho for over 25 years. A graduate of Harvard College and the Johns Hopkins School of Medicine, Dr. LeBow was board certified in two specialties: family practice and preventive medicine. He had extensive experience working on the development of health systems and preventive programs in over 20 developing countries, including a two-year stint as a Peace Corps physician in Bolivia. LeBow, however, devoted most of his career to addressing the problems of health care in the United States. A self-described 'health care activist,' in 1998 and 1999 he was president of Physicians for a National Health Program. After being paralyzed in a cycling accident, he died in late 2003.*

Some of the most onerous paperwork, sad to say, may be for Medicare, although not so much in the office setting. I pity the poor home health and nursing home workers who spend three-quarters of their time writing notes about each patient. They cram endless handwritten notes into tiny writing so that the required information fits in the spaces provided. They can't possibly have much time left to care for the patients. Similarly, RNs in hospitals are consumed with filling in forms or completing notes. That's one of the prime reasons why nursing has lost desirability as a profession. The situation cries out for improvement and simplification.

The eligibility factors of federal and state entitlement programs are quite complex, especially for vulnerable people, those on low incomes, the uninformed, and people with a low level of education. To highlight the effect of the 'eligibility factor,' it is interesting to note what Richard Lamm writes in his book, *The Brave New World of Health Care*:

> The social impact of the Medicaid system in these two states varies considerably. In 1996 if a family of three made over $2,880 in Virginia, they were ineligible for Medicaid, while in Oregon a family of three could earn $12,980 before losing their Medicaid. Thus, Virginia would only pay for health care for this family if they earned under 22 percent of the federal poverty level, while Oregon would cover this family if they earned up to 100 percent of the poverty level. The average nationwide rate is 40 percent.

He went on to add:

> Once a state decides to cover some part of its low-income population, it has to decide a multilateral equation: *what* services to provide to *which* low-income individuals?

> Virginia and Oregon are two examples of the "catch-22" that American public policy inhabits.

The criteria of the eligibility factor has not only produced many anomalies, paradoxes and much paperwork, but has also created hassles for millions of individuals and families as they work their genuine cases through a bureaucratic maze of various state and federally funded entitlement programs. Sometimes it takes years for the bureaucratic machinery to settle individual eligibility cases in these programs, wasting a great deal of human resources and money instead of using them on the quality of the patient's health care.

**Fraud and abuse in entitlement programs**

New controls created in order to cut costs and limit fraud and abuse have led to more paperwork and new demands on administrators and doctors. Physicians complain about all the paperwork required: charts, operative notes, transfer notes, and medical record updates in general. As Dr. Robert LeBow observed, "The new brand of paperwork that has come about with managed care and anti-fraud efforts has added a whole new dimension, including new armies of bureaucratic personnel, to the paperwork nightmare." In *Health Care Meltdown,* he also says:

> When HCFA admitted that it had paid out $23 billion too much through fraudulent or inflated Medicare billings in 1998, people seemed to blame Medicare. But it wasn't Medicare that did

the billings. It was the providers or crooks who submitted the inflated or fraudulent charges.

HCA/Columbia, the nation's largest for-profit hospital chain, systematically overcoded diagnoses to bilk Medicare. This was but one of their questionable practices to maximize their billings. They paid a "first installment" fine of $740 million to Medicare as part of a settlement. Even Illinois Blue Cross paid a fine of $140 million for ripping off Medicare.

Mental health has proven to be a prime profit center (through fraud) for both corporations that have mental health facilities and individuals who run "shelter homes." Some psychiatric hospitals were keeping patients for just as long as their insurance paid the bill, with little regard for the need. Tenet paid a $300 million fine for that practice....

The profit motivation may have led to collusion between the shelter homes and greedy surgeons, who were able to bill Medicare or Medicaid for the procedures whether they were needed or not.

The *Wall Street Journal* reported on May 9, 2006, "Tenet Hospital Faces Ban from Federal Programs. A federal agency is seeking to bar Tenet Healthcare Corp.'s Alvarado Hospital Medical Center from participation in government health-care programs, based on allegations that the San Diego hospital paid kickbacks to doctors in exchange for patient referrals." Previously Tenet paid a $300 million fine. According to the *Wall Street Journal* of June 29, 2006, Tenet Healthcare Corp. was to pay another $725 million to settle allegations that it overcharged the Medicare program from 2000 to 2002.

The Health industry is the fastest growing economy in the U.S., wherein money and profit have become the important and integral factors rather than a patient's health care. The current fragmented health care system in the U.S. is more prone to scandals, greed, and bureaucracy, than the health care systems of other rich countries.

## Prescription drugs PART D for seniors and the disabled

The U.S. Congress passed another entitlement program called Prescription Drugs for seniors, which started the coverage of prescription drugs on January 1, 2006. The Congressional Budget Office estimated that the Medicare prescription drug benefit program (Part D) would cost $792 billion from 2006 to 2015. Medicare prescription drug coverage is insurance that covers both brand name and generic drugs for people eligible for Medicare. Some people call it the greatest advance in health care for seniors since the inception of Medicare in 1965, while others consider this program as deeply flawed and say that it helps drug and insurance companies at the expense of seniors. They further claim the law for prescription drugs was written by the drug companies for the benefit of those companies. Moreover, drug companies are protected from directly negotiating the price of drugs with Medicare, while the Veterans Administration directly negotiates the price of drugs with drug companies. The jury is out whether this fragmented prescription drug bill will succeed or become another albatross in the American health care system.

It is estimated that the federally subsidized prescription drug insurance plan, Part D, is available to 43 million seniors and disabled people. Some 37 million people with Medicare have prescription drug coverage, which includes about 9 million individual enrollees in stand-alone prescription drug plans. According to E.J. Mundell, *HealthDay* reporter, 28 million of those 37 million members had already switched to Part D from existing coverage such as Medicaid, Medicare Advantage, VA benefits, or employer-based plans. The last day of enrollment was May 15, 2006. After that date, enrollees had to pay a penalty in the form of a percentage added to their premiums in order to participate in Part D.

The new Medicare Part D will increase the bottom line profits of drug companies. Richard T Evans, an analyst at Stanford C. Bernstein & Co., said in *Business Week* of October 17, 2005, that he expected the Medicare drug benefit Part D to give a 2–3% boost to drug company earnings in the first two years of the program. He figured, "insurers will offer plans that cover many brand-name drugs in early years to attract people to sign up. That will trigger an increase in the use of drugs by seniors with little in the way of price pressure."

Some of the problems and issues of the new Medicare Part D are as follows.

*What are the choices?* According to the Commonwealth Fund, in 2006 there were nearly 2,200 insurance coverage plans available across the U.S, with premiums ranging from $1.87 to more than $100 a month, with the average premium estimated at $32 per month. In the state of California, there are over 200 plans for drug coverage while San Diego County alone has 45 plans from 19 insurance companies. To most seniors and the disabled the choice of plans is not only confusing but also very frustrating. It is hard to imagine how mind-boggling and bewildering it must be for frail seniors, those with dementia, those with severe disabilities, and people with the least access to information or of limited education, to make an informed choice as to which plan costs the least while still meeting their needs. Did these legislators ask their parents or grandparents about the choices offered in so many plans before passing these bills? It would be interesting to know the opinions of their relatives!

*What is covered?* In 2006, most plans excluded coverage once drug costs exceeded $2,250 in a year, with a maximum yearly deductible of $250. After that, the plan participant was required to spend a total of $3,600 out-of-pocket, which did not include the premium, before they could make further claims. This coverage gap is referred to as 'the doughnut hole.' Some plans either cover the cost of generic drugs within the doughnut hole, or may cover generic and brand name drugs for a substantial monthly premium. Prescription drug coverage is flawed basically, and very disturbing to those who fall into the gap.

*What are the statistics?* Over 43 million people are eligible for prescription drugs under Medicare Part D, which includes seniors and people with disabilities. According to a PBS report on May 8, 2006, nearly 30 million people had participated so far, but most low-income people had still to register. This report suggests that four out of ten people will fall into the doughnut hole, or coverage gap. It is proving much harder to register low-income people and those who may be very old. These groups are hard to reach although they hardly make any co-payments for their prescription drugs. A CNN poll of May 9, 2006, reported that 26% of the participants said that prescription drug Part D was working for them while 46% reported that it was not working, and the rest were undecided.

*Glitches and confusion* occurred when Part D came into operation on January 1, 2006. Some people learned that they no longer had coverage for their medications when they went to their pharmacy, while others could not buy their medications because their names did not appear in the drug plan system on the computer. There were bureaucratic problems such as pharmacists and other callers who could not get through to customer service representatives answering a Part D hotline. There were also problems about payment, with inaccurate and inappropriate information. It is hard to visualize how elderly seniors, the severely disabled or uninformed low-income people could possibly understand, or choose, or even know all the choices in the plans. It caused a great deal of anxiety amongst the most vulnerable groups of American society. After a rocky and confusing start in 2006, the administration sorted out many of the glitches. HHS Secretary Mike Leavitt stated on January 18, 2006, that the government had instructed insurers to cover a thirty-day supply, regardless of whether or not the medications were on the plan's formulary, (a list of approved and covered prescription drugs) and to limit co-payments, but individual states had to bear the cost of this emergency filling of prescriptions for seniors. Any program that is not simple to implement is bound to have problems.

The *San Diego Union-Tribune* of May 8, 2006 reported:

> About 6 million elderly low-income and disabled
> Americans who received drug coverage through

Medicaid (or Medi-Cal in California),the government's health insurance for the poor, were automatically switched to a Medicare drug plan on Jan. 1. The change meant, among other things, that low-income seniors, who had no out-of-pocket expenses under Medi-Cal, would have to pay $1 to $5 in co-payment each time they refill a prescription under their new Medicare drug plans.

There has been aggressive marketing by some insurance companies and their agents to promote their drug plans, which is highly unethical. Insurance companies are rushing in to cover the prescription drug market that covers 43 million seniors and disabled people, as private plans and insurers will deliver the heavily subsidized drug benefit. Large insurance companies that advertised heavily have benefited most in enrolling people into their versions of the offered drug plans. UnitedHealth Group Inc., owners of PacifiCare Health Systems, received the largest share of enrollees (30%) through aggressive marketing. This company signed a lucrative contract with AARP to sell drug plans—AARP being the powerful senior's lobby brand with over 30 million paying members. Humana Inc. had a market share of nearly 20% for drug only plans. Price setting for each drug is solely in the hands of the drug companies. The VA negotiates directly with these companies over the price of each drug, while this is not the case for Medicare Part D. Thus, the drug companies can raise their prices whenever they please. It is a major flaw in the Medicare Part D program.

It is worrisome that there is nothing to stop a private insurance company from removing a drug from its formulary midway through the life of the insurance policy, even though the plan locks a senior or disabled person in for months to come.

Robert Novak of the *Chicago Sun-Times*, a senior himself, wrote in his column that "President Bush's Medicare drug benefit that went into effect January 1, 2006, looks like a political blunder of far-reaching consequences. The hideous complexity of the scheme, which has the effect of discouraging seniors from signing up, is beginning to face difficulties." He went on to add:

> The White House and the House Republican leadership forced the drug benefit down the throats of unhappy conservatives. In a memorable pre-dawn session, resisting Republican House members were threatened with dire consequences, and offered rich awards, as the roll call was held open for more than an hour to erase a 12-vote deficit.

It is not only the lack of viability and the complexity of the program that is noticeable; the program would also add nearly $100 billion a year to the federal budget in the near future.

The Medicare prescription drug program is far too complex, with too many plans, making it almost impossible for most seniors to make the optimum choice for their prescription drug requirements. There are also other key points that should have been included in Medicare Part D legislation and these are:

- The federal government should not have been prohibited from negotiating cheaper drug prices for patients as it has tremendous buying power to settle drug prices with the pharmaceutical industry. The Veterans Administration directly negotiates with the pharmaceutical industry about the price of each drug. Why not allow Medicare to do the same?

- The Department of Health and Human Services imposed a ban on importing safe, prescription drugs from Canada unless they are approved by the Food and Drug Administration (FDA). This bit of legislation protects drug companies. Some institutions, companies, and local governments import prescription drugs from Canada for their employees while thousands of seniors travel to Canada and Mexico to buy drugs that are much cheaper than in the U.S. Why did this legislation protect the drug companies? It was due to their lobbying power!

- The coverage gap, or doughnut hole, is a major flaw in the prescription drug bill, requiring seniors to pay $3600 out-of-pocket after an initial $2,250 of drug coverage under various plans. Experts expect that four out ten seniors and disabled people will fall in the category of the coverage gap. This gap should have been closed in the Medicare Part D bill.

- The prescription drug program is far too complex and adds to the federal budget deficit.

The jury is still out over whether this complex entitlement, Medicare Part D, which costs the federal government nearly an extra $100 billion per year, will succeed with so many flaws if changes, such as fixing the doughnut hole, are not made.

**Advertising and drug companies**

In the Kaiser Family Foundation poll conducted in February 2005, over 70% of people felt that drug companies are more concerned about making profits than developing new drugs and putting patients first. At the same time, a vast majority of Americans believe prescription drugs significantly improve their health and quality of life. This poll also found that a large majority of people want the federal government to curb the rising costs of prescription drugs by regulation.

Drew Altman, Kaiser Foundation President stated, "Rightly or wrongly, drug companies are now the number one villain in the public eye when it comes to rising health care costs." The sliding approval ratings put the pharmaceutical industry in the company of oil companies and managed care organizations in public views.

Prescription drug advertising budgets of pharmaceutical companies, particularly American ones, are increasing at a phenomenal rate in comparison to their research and development budgets. The budget for advertising drugs increased from $5 billion in 1995 to nearly $20 billion in 2005—an increase of 400% in a space of ten years. Dr. Marcia Angell, lecturer at the Harvard

Medical School, said in an interview on September 7, 2004, "the pharmaceutical industry is a vast marketing machine that thrives on monopoly but produces few innovative drugs." She went on to add that the top U.S. drug makers spend two and a half times as much on marketing and administration as they do on research. Universities or small biotech companies discovered at least a third of the drugs marketed by industry leaders, but the cost to the public is still inflated. She cites the example of Taxol, the cancer drug discovered by the National Institutes of Health (NIH), but sold by Bristol-Myers Squibb for $20,000 a year, reportedly twenty times the manufacturing cost. The company paid the NIH only 0.5% in royalties for the drug. This is a common story of how large drug companies benefit enormously from drugs produced by smaller companies and how these major drug companies take advantage of drug research done at universities and other research institutes.

According to Dr. Angell, the top ten companies in the pharmaceutical industry made more profits than the rest of the Fortune 500 companies in 2003.

Pfizer has become the largest drug company in the world through acquisitions and the introduction of several blockbuster drugs like Celebrex and Lipitor. It is the most aggressive marketer of drugs, to both doctors and consumers, with a $3 billion advertising budget. Pfizer had an army of 38,000 global sales representatives with a domestic sales force of over 11,000 people in January of 2005. Small drug companies seek alliances with Pfizer because of its marketing muscle. Sometimes two of the company's sales representatives see the same doctor to promote a drug in the same day. The *Wall Street Journal* reported on February 11, 2005, that Pfizer plans to cut about $2 billion in costs and to overhaul how it markets drugs to doctors. However, will the drug companies refrain from aggressive marketing of prescription drugs? The answer is no unless the Food and Drug Administration (FDA) takes effective regulatory measures to control the distorted drug advertisements of these companies. Shamelessly, in 2009 some drug companies have even begun direct-mail marketing of prescription drugs to consumers.

The following table gives some interesting aspects of drug company's aggressive marketing practices.

Figure 14

| Amount drug companies agreed to pay the U.S. since 2001 to settle allegations of illegal sales and marketing practices | **$2 billion** |
|---|---|
| Increase in total spending on drug promotion in the U.S. from 1997 to 2002 | **93%** |
| Increase in spending on domestic Research and Development in the same period | **66%** |
| Increase from 1995 to 2000 in marketing staff at brand-name drug companies | **59%** |
| Decrease from 1995 to 2000 in R. and D. staff at brand-name drug companies | **2%** |

Source: *Time* Magazine July 5, 2004.

Many pharmaceutical companies had to withdraw hyped advertisement campaigns for prescription drugs as the ads either pitched misleading information or were simply open to ridicule. A House of Representatives committee reported in May 2005, that more than 3,000 sales representatives gave doctors misleading information about Vioxx's (anti-inflammatory drug) risks. Merck Inc., producer of Vioxx was forced to recall the drug when a study showed that patients taking this drug for eighteen months had doubled their risk of heart attacks. Nearly 10,000 lawsuits had been filed against Merck, seeking billions of dollars in damages and accusing the company of misleading doctors and the feds, according to an article in *Forbes* of May 8, 2006. Several cases had already reached the courts, with some decisions going against Merck.

The Food and Drug Administration forced Pfizer to withdraw two television advertisements for Viagra, its medicine for erectile dysfunctional, stating the ads overstated Viagra's effectiveness. Pfizer also withdrew advertisements for Celebrex, its best selling arthritis pain reliever, when studies showed high doses were associated with an increased risk of heart attacks. Pfizer has withdrawn the aggressive marketing campaign for its blockbuster cholesterol-lowering drug Lipitor as well, and the painkiller Bextra was taken off the market on April 7, 2005. The FDA ordered nineteen popular prescription drugs from Celebrex, to Mobic, to high-dose Naproxen, to carry tough new warnings about the increased risk of heart attack and strokes.

TAP Pharmaceutical Products paid $875 million to federal authorities as a settlement in 2001 for kickback schemes to get doctors to prescribe its prostrate cancer drug Lupron.

Congress eased advertising restrictions on prescription drugs in 1997. Since then many ad campaigns for drugs have caused people to question their validity. It seems that many pharmaceutical advertising executives have buried their heads in the sand and persist in marketing prescription drugs as if they were products like cars, clothing, or perfume— producing ads that seem full of vitality, sexiness and whatever other spin they can think of, in order to induce demand from patients. In short, many drug companies mislead people about the effectiveness of their drugs.

Robert Langreth and Matthew Harper wrote an excellent article that appeared in *Forbes* on May 8, 2006, with the headline "Pill Pushers—How the Drug Industry Abandoned Science for Salesmanship," The authors of this article state advertisement budgets, sales, and the claims made in drug ads in the following chart.

Figure 15

| Lamisil (Novartis) | Toenail fungus | Ad budget (2005) $110 million | U.S. Sales $538 million |
|---|---|---|---|
| Levitra (Bayer, GSK, Schering-Plough) | Erectile dysfunction | Ad budget $50 million | U.S. Sales $150 million |
| Lunesta (Sepracor) | Insomnia | Ad Budget (2005) $215 million | U.S. Sales $329 million |
| Nexium (AstraZeneca) | Heartburn | Ad budget $226 million | U.S. Sales $3.1 billion |
| Crestor (AstraZeneca) | High Cholesterol | Ad budget $142 million | U.S. Sales $730 million |

Source: TNS Media Intelligence (ad budget); company statements; FDA
Novartis disputes Lamisil budget and Lunesta budget is only for the first 9
months.

According to the authors of "Pushing Pills," drug companies have tripled the ranks of their sales people to 100,000—that is one seller for every nine doctors. They said:

> Even the research lab is more market-driven than ever. More than $9 billion a year in research spending goes to clinical trials of drugs that are already approved or may soon be—often to snare new ad slogans. That is up 90% in four years, says Goldman Sachs. Some of these ad-driven trials are skewed to pit the sponsor's full-strength product against a weaker dose of a rival pill.

The authors went on to say that slogan driven trials feed an explosion of drug ads aimed at the consumer, and added,

> TV spots ply supposed low-risk, quick fixes to millions of people: Try Zoloft to get happy;

gobble a state-of-the-art pain pill when aspirin would work fine. Drugs designed for narrow sets of patients end up in the hands of a far broader audience. "It creates demand where there's not even disease there," complains internist Robert Centor of the University of Alabama.

Any intelligent or educated person knows that all medicines have side effects.

It is reported that drug companies not only provide extensive research grants to doctors in various universities and institutes so that the doctors or researchers can vouch for the credibility of their drug's effectiveness, but that extensive gifts are lavished upon these people too. Drug companies also use ghostwriters in order to advance their drugs according to an article by Anna Wilde Mathews of the *Wall Street Journal.* She wrote:

> It's an example of an open secret in medicine: Many of the articles that appear in scientific journals under the bylines of prominent academics are actually written by ghostwriters in the pay of drug companies. These seemingly objective articles, which doctors around the world use to guide their care of patients, are often part of a marketing campaign by companies to promote a product or play up the condition it treats.

The following extract from an article by Dan Vergano, "Study: Medical Manual's Authors Often Tied to Drug Makers," published in *USA Today* in April 2006, sums up simply the cozy relationships that exist between researchers, doctors, and administrators, and the drug companies:

> A majority of the medical experts who created the "bible" for diagnosing mental illness have undisclosed financial links to drug-makers, says a study out today.

And some panels overseeing disorders that require treatment with prescription drugs, such as schizophrenia and "mood disorders," were 100% filled with experts financially tied to the pharmaceutical industry, says the study published in the journal *Psychotherapy and Psychosomatics.*

The Diagnostic and Statistical Manual for Mental Disorders (DSM) is the American Psychiatric Association's diagnosis manual. It is also used as the basis for insurance payments for psychiatric treatments, including drugs. "No blood tests exist for the disorders in the DSM, it relies on the judgments from practitioners who rely on the manual," says lead study author Lisa Cosgrove of the University of Massachusetts, Boston.

The researchers looked for research funds, consultancies, patents, and other gifts or grants received by members of the 18 separate DSM preparation panels from 1989 to 2004, both before and after their terms. They found that among the 170 medical experts who created the two most recent editions of the manual, 56% had one or more financial ties to the pharmaceutical industry. In addition to the schizophrenia and mood disorder panels' links, more than 80% of the panel members for "anxiety disorders," "eating disorders," "medication-induced movement disorders" and "premenstrual dysphonic disorder" had financial ties.

Such stories must lead to the conclusion that drug companies use unethical advertising techniques and market aggressively through a combination of sophisticated and corrupt practices in order to create demand for their drugs. Vergano also referred to an article by Barbara Mintzes that appeared in the *PLoS Medicine* journal in April 2006, saying it "accused the drug industry of 'disease mongering'—inventing diseases from everyday aggravations such as 'restless legs,'—and of widening definitions of diseases to sweep up more patients."

The following points have been the main cause of double-digit inflation in the price of prescription drugs over the past ten years. Lobbyists for drug companies have played a key role in indirectly corrupting legislators.

- Spending on advertisements for drugs has increased by over 400% in the last ten years, while new drug approvals by the FDA have declined by nearly 250% in the same period.

- There are aggressive drug marketing ads with considerable hype, paid for by pharmaceutical companies. Drug companies create demand for their drugs when there is neither disease, nor need for that particular drug.

- Budgets for ads have increased by 400%, while there is no comparable increase in researching new drugs.

- Cozy relationships exist between the drug companies and some researchers, doctors, administrators, and legislators.

**Lobbyists and their influence on officials and legislators**

Lobbyists spent over $3 billion trying to influence the federal government by the end of 2004. Expenditure by lobbyists has doubled in the last six years, according to a study by the non-partisan Center for Public Integrity. Corporations, labor unions, interest groups, and individuals, who have served the administration and past legislators, form the main body of lobbyists. According to *PoliticalMoneyLine (PML),* the online organization that tracks lobbying and campaign money, there were 27,765 registered lobbyists at the end of 2005.

There are at least two lobbyists in health care related fields for each elected official in Washington. Health care is one of the most lobbied issues, with over $300 million spent, on average, by lobbyists in the years 2003 to 2005. AARP, the seniors group with Medicare and Social Security concerns, had a lobbying expenditure of $27.8 million, and led other organizations in spending, according to PML. AARP actively promoted the Prescription Drugs Plan, Part D for seniors. *PML* reported lobbyist spending of an incredible $194 million per month, almost $6.5 million a day, or more than $540,000 an hour for a twelve-hour day of lobbying Congress and the executive branch!

Money talks! The amount of money spent by lobbyists on influencing the U.S. Congress and the executive branch is neither healthy for democracy, nor is it helpful in drafting legislation in Congress, especially any legislation that concerns health care. There is no other rich democratic country in the world in which citizens would allow that kind of influence by lobbyists.

Lobbyists from pharmaceutical and insurance companies, and from attorneys and doctors organizations, contribute money to the campaign coffers of legislators from both parties. They also exert influence on the executive branch and the staff of key legislators by discreetly lavishing them with gifts and other perks. Many drug and insurance industry lobbyists often conduct their operations behind the mask of communications and legal firms, making it hard to know how much these companies actually spend in their attempts to influence government officials. Drug and insurance companies reportedly influenced the writing and passage of Medicare Part D.

Dana Wilkie of the Copley News Service wrote in the *San Diego Union-Tribune*:

> The passage of the prescription drug plan—which seniors across the country are slamming for its confusion, high costs, and capriciousness—comes with accounts of strong-arm tactics to push it through the House by pharmaceutical and health care companies showering campaign gifts on key lawmakers, and cozy arrangements for those who wrote the bill, and then departed for lucrative jobs as lobbyists.

Many representatives of pharmaceutical companies, and of the insurance and health care industries, acknowledge that lobbyists try to bend lawmakers' ears but they contend that their impact on policymakers tends to be exaggerated. Common sense says that if a person pays you in some form, then you are more likely to listen to that person and return the favor.

The stories of Jack Abramoff, former lobbyist, and Randy "Duke" Cunningham, the former Republican Representative from Rancho Santa Fe, only highlight in an exaggerated manner how lobbyists influence legislators to win favors for their clients' pet projects. Duke received a ten-year prison sentence after pleading guilty to several charges, and Abramoff faced trial and a long prison term after pleading guilty to fraud, tax evasion, and conspiracy charges. Some legislators, or members of their staff, are caught in these lobbyist relationships of influence peddling, while many others tend to hide behind cozy relationships of money and gifts from lobbyists in exchange for favors from them, and from the executive branch. Why otherwise, would there be so many lobbyists based in Washington?

The influence peddling of Duke and Abramoff might seem far removed from the average voter, but Medicare Part D is not. The influence of lobbyists, especially from drug and insurance companies, really comes through in the bill. Dana Wilkie wrote in her analysis that "Americans complain that the new insurance sometimes pays for one drug but not another, or that they are automatically placed in plans that don't pay for their prescriptions. There is anger about delayed access to drugs and frustration over complex provisions."

Most of the media gives an easy ride to major drug companies for their absurd advertisements because ads bring in money for the television and media companies; hence, it is difficult for them to criticize companies that bring them substantial revenues. The media almost never criticizes drug companies for their role in drug ads and their influence in exerting pressure on legislators. It is also noticeable that PBS does not use drug-company advertising, while other TV stations are quite content to put up with hyped prescription drug ads.

Ted Koppel of *News Night*, soon after leaving the show, indicated that many advertisers wanted to influence the content of reporting. This is surely an unhealthy sign.

## Health insurance industry and insurance policies

Customers (state and federal governments, companies, and small businesses) of the health insurance industry have seen premium rates rise by double-digits since the year 2000. This rate only slightly slowed down to the 7–8% range in 2005. Major health insurers are enjoying healthy returns on the policies they deliver to consumers. The higher costs of health insurance are justified by insurers as they point out the higher cost of medical equipment, bigger payments for doctors, more tests for patients' symptoms, and the ever-rising cost of prescription drugs. Even the federal government approved substantially larger rebates to health insurers for elderly clients receiving Medicare in 2004.

Health insurers have a great deal of leverage in their operations. Firstly, they do not have to finance inventory, and secondly, they receive premiums in advance and pay out later. Health care insurers have no long-term liabilities, unlike other industries, and their obligations last for no longer than a year. The capital demands in health care are great, but they are mostly the responsibility of hospitals and laboratories.

Top executives of health insurance companies receive exorbitant salaries and remunerations from their companies. The *Economist* reported on June 12, 2004, that William McGuire, head of UnitedHealth Group of Minnesota, earned $30 million in pay in 2003, and exercised $84 million in stock options from earlier years. This left him with further options worth $840 million in 2003. McGuire's number two, Stephen Hemsley, earned $13.7 million in compensation and held further stock options worth $350 million. John Rowe, the head of Aetna, earned $16 million, Larry Glasscock of Anthem made $51 million, and Leonard Schaeffer of WellPoint made $27 million. This level of compensation for top executives is obscene in a health care industry, where the main concern should be to provide the best health care possible for the residents of the United States, and to do it in a cost effective manner.

Lavish remunerations in an industry like health care, which receives a fair amount of taxpayer money from state and federal governments, require tougher controls and regulations from authorities in order to control the rising cost of health care insurance. There is no chance of health insurers regulating themselves as long as the current health care system in America exists.

The diversity of private health insurance is amazing. In this respect, no other country in the world provides such a selection of policies to chose from, all with varying deductibles. Over 1,500 health insurers handle this market. There are also policies for prescription drugs for seniors and disabled people. In the state of California alone, there are nearly 150 combinations of prescription drug policies and deductible amounts. The Health and Human Services Department reported that about 11.5 million elderly and disabled people signed up for the Medicare Part D prescription drug benefit by the enrollment date of May 15, 2006, which brought the number of beneficiaries to 38.7 million. This left about 4 to 5 million beneficiaries without prescription drug insurance coverage.

There is nothing to stop a private health insurance company from removing a drug from its formulary midway through the life of an insurance policy, even though a senior or a disabled person is locked into the plan for months to come. Such are the advantages enjoyed by insurance companies at the expense of patients and clients.

The rising cost of health insurance has led to limited health plans by insurers, medical discount cards, and cross-border insurance policies in the border states of California, Arizona, Texas, and New Mexico.

Insurance companies have introduced low cost plans, sometimes called 'mini-medical' or 'limited plans.' These plans are catching on as employers struggle to restrain the rising cost of health insurance. Most of the limited health plans cover drugs and visits to the doctor's office, but very little hospitalization. Employers and the self-employed increasingly turn to these more affordable types of health insurance, which limit benefits to cover only routine services, lab work, and medications, but provide little coverage for hospital or emergency care. These plans often cap annual payouts at $10,000 or less, and may not cover major illnesses and catastrophes.

Insurance companies have also started to provide cross-border health insurance policies in states bordering Mexico. California passed legislation in 1998 and 1999 legalizing and regulating cross-border HMOs. These health insurance plans are much cheaper for both employers and employees. Patients see approved doctors and get treatment in Tijuana and Mexicali, in Mexico. Patients' treatment costs are less than one fifth of those in the United States. Only U.S. citizens or Mexican citizens living in America can sign up for these plans offered by California insurers. According to Sarah Skidmore, staff writer for the *San Diego Union-Tribune,* in her article of October16, 2005, such plans had over 150,000 California workers enrolled in them in the year 2005. Their popularity in the states bordering Mexico is bound to increase as the cost of health care and insurance keeps rising in the United States.

Companies that provide so called 'discount cards' have proliferated. In an article of December 26, 2005, in *Business Week*, Aaron Bernstein and Joseph Weber stated, "Many discount card companies offer valid savings on services such as doctors' visits and prescription medicines. But, because they typically aren't selling insurance, they're usually not regulated by state insurance commissioners, creating an opening for scammers." They went on to add that as many as 17% of the United States' 40 million temporary and part-time workers—7 million people—say they have health insurance when they actually have discount cards.

Many of the discount card companies operate through internet websites that they advertise in the media. The company reps have very limited contact with their clients, communicating either by telephone or in writing. A rep from one of these companies who called me, stated that the health 'insurance policy' he was selling was cheap because the paperwork of filling out forms could be done online, avoiding the need to send any information or forms to the consumer's home address. There are also the following rip-offs by 'discount cards.'

- Discount cards are not health insurance; therefore, they are not strictly regulated by state insurance commissioners.

- Discount card companies often market the cards as 'health plans' and 'deductibles'; this leads to misleading ads, which can lead consumers to think that they are buying real health insurance.

- Many doctors and hospitals do not honor discount cards, but companies may still list them in their participant schemes.

- Many discount card companies require credit card or bank information, and they may still bill consumers after they have cancelled the cards.

- Some of the companies may deal with the consumer in only an online basis, which may put pressure on consumers to buy discount cards online.

Vince DiBenedetto, CEO of Chicago-based Coverdell & Co., a unit of Vertrue Inc., a publicly traded marketing company, estimated that there are nearly 20 million discount card holders in America. Coverdell alone has more than 3.5 million cardholders.

All of these problems with discount card companies have arisen because the cost of health insurance has become unbearable for the insured and the uninsured in the United States.

Insurance companies can also deny health insurance to seriously ill patients or those with pre-existing medical conditions. Therefore, such patients can only rely on state and federal programs for their treatment, and in some cases on charitable organizations or trusts. This leads to insecurity among those patients who are at the mercy of state or federal authorities if they are unable to locate a charitable organization that can pay for their health treatment.

The lawyers of the respective companies write the insurance policies, which run into tens of pages, and which consumers do not usually understand. My nephew is a good example. He is in his twenties, well educated, and has a health insurance policy with Blue Shield. He had difficulty reading his policy and simply signed the forms without understanding his coverage. Most consumers do not understand what their coverage is, nor do they read their policies because of all the legal jargon used. In the case of disputes, the interpretation of the policy is in the hands of lawyers. It becomes a mutually beneficial arrangement between lawyers and insurance companies. The complexity of policies leads to litigation on behalf of contestants.

In summary, the following is necessary to cut down on the cost of health insurance:

- Companies must provide policies written in plain English. They should be required to provide only two or three forms that outline their policies and deductibles clearly.

- Allow only a limited number of companies to provide health insurance in each state by using a bidding process and selecting the top three companies.

- Do not allow insurance companies to exclude people, such as those with pre-existing medical conditions, from their health insurance policies.

Competition is preserved by following the above process.

**Bankruptcies**

The American health care system is a major cause of personal bankruptcies in the United States. Costly illnesses trigger half of them, according to findings from a Harvard University study released on February 2, 2005. Estimates put the number caused by people unable to pay their medical bills at over one million. The journal *Health Affairs* published the results of the study online

"Unless you're Bill Gates, you're just one serious illness away from bankruptcy," said Dr. David Himmelstein, the study's lead author and an associate professor of medicine. He added, "Most of the medically bankrupt were average Americans who happened to get sick."

According to this study, questionnaires were given to 1,771 bankruptcy filers in the states of California, Illinois, Pennsylvania, Tennessee, and Texas in 2001. More than 900 of those questioned cited health care expenses as the main cause of their financial problems. There were 1.46 million bankruptcies in the U.S. in 2001. The study also estimated that medically caused bankruptcies actually affect 2 million Americans each year, counting debtors and their dependents, including 700,000 children.

"We need to rethink health reform," said Dr. Steffie Woolhandler, a study co-author and associate professor of medicine at Harvard. "Covering the uninsured is not enough. We must also upgrade and guarantee continuous coverage for those who have insurance." The entire study gave an interesting insight into the deficiencies of the American health care system.

Jeff Morris, resident scholar at the American Bankruptcy Institute, founded by Congress in 1982 to analyze bankruptcy trends, stated that the Harvard study confirmed ABI findings of 1996, in which 57% of bankruptcy filers cited medical problems as the primary cause.

In the rich countries of Europe, and in Japan, Australia, and Canada, bankruptcy is an exception for a person unfortunate enough to fall victim to a severe illness. Human beings are the biggest resource of a nation, and these countries consider health care as a basic need. It is shameful that America, the richest country in the world, can allow its people to face bankruptcy because of an inadequate health care system.

**Doctors, lawyers, and malpractice lawsuits**

The fear of getting sued is leading doctors to practice more 'defensive medicine,' i.e., ordering excessive tests, avoiding risky procedures, and referring patients to other expert doctors, in order to assure that they have the correct diagnosis of a patient's condition, as well as the best possible remedy for the particular diagnosis. In itself, there is nothing wrong with practicing defensive medicine, but when this becomes routine for confirming even the simplest diagnosis of a patient, then the cost of health care rises and it becomes a waste of the American health care system's resources.

In a study published in the June 2005 edition of the *Journal of the American Medical Association*, 93% of Pennsylvania doctors surveyed in 2003 reported that they sometimes or often practiced defensive medicine because of malpractice concerns.

The problem of overly prescribing drugs to the old and the very young has drawn widespread attention. Constance Holden observed in *Science Now Daily News* in 2007, that the average American over the age of sixty-five is "taking eight kinds of drugs and ordering 27 refills a year." At the other end of the spectrum 'diseases' like juvenile bipolar disorder, attention deficit disorder, and childhood depression are now treated routinely with drug therapy, although these conditions were not recognized as diseases 60 years ago. This is another example of how medicine is prescribed by doctors as a security measure to ensure against lawsuits.

Another study, conducted by David Studdert of the Harvard School of Public Health, found that about 40% of the medical malpractice cases filed in the United States are frivolous, and that groundless cases sometimes pit trial lawyers against doctors, with lawmakers in the middle. The study also concluded that there was no evidence of medical error, nor that the patient had sustained any injury, in many of the lawsuits. Mr. Studdert found that "The system did reasonably well in sorting the good claims from the bad ones." Groundless lawsuits still accounted for 15% of the money paid out in settlements or verdicts. A major problem in the American health care system is the fact that there are so many groundless cases filed in America.

Litigation has not only increased the cost of malpractice insurance, but has induced many doctors to leave their medical practices altogether. In a speech before doctors and medical workers in St Louis in January 2005, President Bush called attention to a neurosurgeon that was on the stage with him. The doctor, the President said, was paying $265,000 a year in premiums against malpractice claims. Bush also complained about the skyrocketing cost of 'junk lawsuits' against doctors and hospitals. Dr. Thomas, an ENT specialist whom I knew for more than twenty years, frequently complained to me about paying more than $200,000 a year for malpractice insurance in New Jersey. He worked very hard, with two private practice clinics and the chair of a local hospital. He made nearly a million dollars a year, and loved his work. Unfortunately, he died of colon cancer in 2002.

Reports say that South Florida has the most expensive rates for malpractice insurance in the country. Some obstetricians and general surgeons there paid nearly $280,000 for coverage in 2004. Nebraska had the least expensive rates in the country, where obstetricians paid $16,194 for coverage in that same year. In a sparsely populated state like Nebraska, there were very few frivolous lawsuits, which helped to lower premiums.

Some blame insurance companies for the price gouging of malpractice insurance premiums, but others blame lawyers for filing groundless lawsuits. Over 60% of the lawyers in the world live in the U.S., while the U.S. makes up only 5% of the world population. America is the most litigious country in the world. Hence, some in the legal profession are bound to indulge in filing frivolous lawsuits.

In an article in the *Economist* of December 17, 2005, titled "Scalpel, Scissors, Lawyer—Health-care Litigation Costs America Far Too Much", the magazine reports:

> Trial lawyers argue that malpractice lawsuits deter negligence. Craig Dickman, an obstetrician affiliated to CWC, says they mostly deter the kind of behavior that might get you sued, which is not the same thing. To cover himself, he says, he orders excessive tests, monitoring, and consultations with specialists. He guesses that 12% to 15% of the procedures he bills for are unnecessary. If he fails to order every imaginable test, even if there is "no clinical evidence of efficacy," he is exposed if something were to go wrong. A trial lawyer can scour the country for the one expert who thinks that his omission might have caused the patient's injury.

Furthermore, the *Economist* reported:

> James Copland of the Centre for Legal Policy at the conservative Manhattan Institute, author of a

recent study called "Trial Lawyers Inc", estimates that the total costs, direct and indirect, of health-care litigation (including suits against doctors, drug firms, HMOs, nursing homes, and so on) could be as much as $200 billion—a Hurricane Katrina every year. This figure involves some heroic extrapolation, but even half that sum would seem a lot to pay for a system that is not even good at compensating patients who are injured.

The previous report really sums up the dilemma that doctors, lawyers, and insurance companies will face if the current health care system in America is not completely overhauled. It is clear that many doctors and lawyers, as well as insurance and drug companies, have become part of the vicious circle that is leading to the ever-increasing cost of health insurance, while patients pay the heavy price of a flawed health care system.

Even the present health care system in America could be more cost effective with the implementation of the following points.

- Only allow a limited number of insurance companies, with two or three policies, to operate in each state. Companies can bid for each type of fixed premium health insurance policy and the first three that bid the lowest premiums can then operate their plans in the states they win in, for a period of three to five years before bidding is renewed.

- Require law partners or lawyers to pay for the cost of bringing frivolous lawsuits if their cases are dismissed, and put a cap on damages awarded in any particular case. Use a fixed schedule for non-economic compensation, instead of judges or jurors picking a figure from the air. Form specialized courts where the judges are experts in complex health care problems and patient conditions–thus excluding juries from hearing complex health care cases—and guarantee patients at least 50% of the awards in any particular case.

- Deal with malpractice cases against doctors, health care employees, and hospitals, at state and local levels first, using ethical review committees comprised of people of integrity, including doctors and lawyers, before allowing cases to proceed.

- Have each state establish a special fund to support patients struck by a catastrophic illness or condition, to prevent personal bankruptcies in these unfortunate circumstances. Require insurance companies to contribute a certain percentage to this fund from insurance premiums.

## Other problems, issues, and mistakes made in the delivery of health care

America has some of the finest hospitals in the world, contributing to high quality research and to educating qualified and competent doctors and nurses. Despite having mostly top quality personnel administering health care, nearly 100,000 patients die each year because of mistakes made by staff working at hospitals. These mistakes are mostly in the form of the wrong dose of medicine, the wrong medicine given to a patient, infection through intravenous feeding tubes, simply not cleansing hands and/or instruments before examining patients, assigning wrong labels to patients, or some form of negligence due to overwork or tiredness. Despite having all of the advantages of a rich country, almost everyone knows someone who has had a bad experience in the American health care system.

David Brown of the *Washington Post* wrote on June 15, 2006:

> Emergency medical care in the United States is on the verge of collapse, with the nation's declining number of emergency rooms dangerously overcrowded and often unable to provide the expertise needed to treat seriously ill people in a safe and efficient manner.

That's the grim conclusion of the three reports
released by the Institute of Medicine yesterday,
the product of an extensive two year look at
emergency care.

The cost of health care goes up as more and more patients
crowd emergency rooms, largely because over 47 million people
are uninsured. These people only rush to the emergency room
when they find that they may have some serious problem with their
health, or because of an emergency created through an accident.
Too often uninsured people live in fear and ignore the initial signs
of a health problem. A middle class acquaintance of mine vomited
and suffered stomach pains for a week. He thought he had food
poisoning. He did not go to see a doctor when the problem arose
because he was uninsured. When the pain became acute he ended
up in an emergency room with acute appendicitis, which required an
immediately operation. He nearly died. The hospital later sent him a
bill for over $60,000.

Too many single mothers do not consult the doctor regularly
during pregnancy, the reason being that they have no insurance.
Only when a severe problem arises, do they end up seeing the
doctor. It is one of the main reasons for the high infant mortality
rate of seven deaths per thousand infants below the age of one, in
the United States. On average, the infant mortality rate of the rich
European countries, and of Japan and Australia, is half that of the
United States.

Millions of Americans have stories to tell about their fears
of not seeing a doctor in time because of being uninsured or even
underinsured, and of the resulting burden of hospital bills that they
could not afford to pay. More than half of the uninsured owe money
to hospitals, and collection agencies pursue a third of them. Delaying
care for fear of medical bills is a downward spiral that leads to
ultimately higher health costs for everyone in the United States.

The high cost of emergency room treatment is well known
among politicians and health administrators, and they are also aware
of the fears of the uninsured and underinsured, yet they have not
addressed these problems in health care.

Medicaid is becoming a growing financial burden for the states that provide health insurance to 52 million low income Americans. Medicaid cost has risen by nearly 50% since 2000 and exceeded $300 billion a year in 2005. According to the non-profit Center for Health Care Strategies, adults with chronic illnesses represent 40% of Medicaid recipients, but 8% of its expenditure. Hospital fees for these patients make up a major chunk of the costs.

There are huge problems and costs for long term and chronically ill patients who are unable to pay their bills, and for the poor who are not insured or simply relying on Medicaid. It would take more than a book to tell all the terrible stories about the health care that this section of society receives. Various media sources and journals have documented this subject well. In some ways, providing home based nursing services would better handle the problem of these long-term care and chronically ill patients, rather than having them occupy the beds of hospitals and other institutions. This could contribute to lessening the cost of Medicaid.

**The role and use of information technology**

Paperwork, inefficient communications, and bureaucracy, riddle the American health care system. In some estimates, it costs as much as 25–30% of the total health care expenditure of over $2 trillion. The use of information technology (IT) could considerably cut down on the cost of health care, even in the present uncoordinated and fragmented system in the U.S.

Dr. David J. Brailer is the National Coordinator of Health Care IT in the Health & Human Services Dept. He has a vision and is a strong advocate for transforming health care through the extensive use of IT, thus cutting down costs. In 2005, a group of CEOs organized by Dr. Brailer's office, including FedEx's Smith and PepsiCo's Reinemund, believed that using IT would cut nearly 30% of U.S health care spending.

Senator Hillary Rodham Clinton and former House Speaker Newt Gingrich jointly advocated bipartisan legislation on electronic health care records for everyone in the United States. A bill like this would certainly save lives by replacing inefficient paper based patient records with a confidential electronic network of health information for each patient.

It could also cut down on medical mistakes from illegible prescriptions written by doctors. They usually have poor handwriting, a fact that is noticeable all around the world! In an efficient IT health care system, patient records would be instantaneously available to health care providers. However, some opponents to the extensive use of IT are worried about patient privacy rights.

If there was a state and national health care network that provided information about each patient, both health care workers and doctors could easily see what drugs each patient was taking, and could then discontinue any drug that might be causing serious problems. In such a network, an individual's health information would be easily accessible, even when a person moved from one county or state, to another.

Most of the billing and administrative tasks in the health care industry are already being handled by IT processes. There is a need for a secure health care network that contains the information of each patient in the United States, and which is only accessible to appropriate health care staff. It is also worth considering the possibility of placing a chip under the skin of newborn children, to carry their health information wherever they go.

*It is not beyond the realm of the richest country in the world to devise a health care network with adequate security and privacy considerations; one which could significantly cut down on the cost of health care, cut down on paperwork, reduce medical errors, and improve the quality of care.*

## Myths and misconceptions

The 2000 World Health Organization (WHO) report on the world's health care systems ranked the United States thirty-seven overall. America also scored low in certain categories such as fairness, where it ranked fifty-four, tied with Fiji. However, the United States was number one by a large margin in per capita spending on health care. These are facts deliberately not mentioned by many policy makers and politicians, in order to hide their failed health care policies, as they continue to talk about what is positive in the American health care system.

Although America has some of the finest institutions, technology, doctors, and health care for those who can afford to pay for it; it is also true that the United States is unique amongst the rich nations, in that it has a fragmented, inefficient, and bureaucratically wasteful system that excludes over 47 million uninsured people from health care. This situation has led to myths and misconceptions about the health care system.

Dr. Robert H. LeBow elaborated on these myths in an elegant manner in his book, *Health Care Meltdown: Confronting the Myths and Fixing Our Failing System*, which is compulsory reading for anyone interested in having input into advancing the cause of universal health care in America. I have taken some of his points, and introduced further perceptions and myths that have a serious bearing on the ability of America to change from managed competition to a universal health care system with built in competition that benefits the entire population.

*America has the best health care system in the world.* The question is for whom, only for the rich? The rich can also get the best health care in any other country in the world! Facts about the American health care system do not come anywhere near to supporting this statement that some politicians and policy makers quote.

*Anyone in America has access to health care by going to an emergency room (ER).* This is true, but most people visit the emergency room only when they are in severe pain or their condition has become acute. Many emergency room patients have to pay very high costs for that form of health care; some of these patients may become bankrupt, as they are unable to pay their medical bills. There is always a 'fear factor' for the uninsured and the underinsured.

*The insured subsidize the uninsured and underinsured in the health care system.* According to Dr. LeBow, "This used to be true, but it's often the opposite today." He added, quoting Donald W. Light:

> The uninsured and people with individual insurance are now substantially subsidizing the care of those with group insurance plans. "Hospitals, clinics, labs and physicians charge individuals [including the uninsured] about four to five times as much as their regular negotiated fees with plans and insurers. [And] insurance companies charge [individuals] much higher premiums for less coverage on the argument that they are at serious risk when they insure one person at a time."

People who receive health insurance through their employers also enjoy the benefit of not paying tax on the employer paid portion of the premiums, which equates to tax-free income. These subsidies are not available to the uninsured or those who have to purchase insurance on their own.

*Socialized health care is bad. The idea works everywhere else in the world, but in America, it will not.* The term 'socialized medicine' has a negative perception amongst people in the United States, because most of them (including those involved in the health care field) are very ignorant of the health care systems of other rich countries. The publicly funded entitlement programs of Medicare, Medicaid, the VHA, the Medicare Part D Prescription Drug Benefit, and many of the state programs, fit the general classification of socialized medicine. These entitlement programs form nearly 50% of the cost of health care in America. Other rich countries also have private sector health care, but not to the same extent as the United States have. Americans are convinced that private solutions are always better than public solutions, but the American private health care system is not working.

*Canada's health care system is terrible, it is failing, and has long waiting lists for certain operations.* Most Americans will dismiss, for the most part, the mainly publicly funded Canadian health care system. The American media, and some policy makers, have succeeded in campaigns to discredit the Canadian system because it has waiting lists for particular operations, but it is still a universal health care system covering everyone and providing easy access to health care. The residents of Canada have no fear of seeing a doctor when a medical problem develops. If the Canadian health care system is terrible, then why do Canadians have longer life spans and much lower infant mortality rates than Americans have? People in Canada have lower rates of heart disease and cancer than people in America have. Many Americans living in states that border Canada buy their prescription drugs in Canadian pharmacies, because drugs there are much cheaper than in the United States.

*Many people come to the United States for health care.* I am unable to find any data that can support this statement. Yes, many rich people from either poor or Arab countries have come to the United States because of a medical condition, but most such patients now go to other rich countries for medical treatment since the 9/11 incident.

*Americans will not accept health care rationing as people have in other countries.* However, health care rationing exists in the United States, as more than 47 million people are uninsured, and millions more are underinsured. 'Rationing' and 'socialized medicine' are only catchwords used by some politicians, policy makers, drug companies, and the media, to create negative reactions within the U.S. population. Rationing health care is already a part of the American health care system. Dr. LeBow wrote, "The definition of U.S.-style rationing is: (a) if you can afford it, you can get it; (b) if you can't afford it, you either can't or won't get it unless (c) it's a dire emergency and (d) you're lucky enough to catch the problem in time and survive."

*Americans will not accept a universal health care system or America cannot afford one.* A majority of Americans is beginning to accept the idea of having a universal health care system that insures everyone in the United States, and all recent polls indicate that people would support a universal system. This has come with the constant increase in the number of uninsured and underinsured, and the ever-increasing cost of health care. Almost every adult knows someone, a friend, acquaintance, or family member, who has had some sort of bad experience with the current system in America. Many policymakers and executives of health related industries reinforce the myth that Americans will not accept universal health care. They see advantages for continuing the status quo with its opportunities for profit. Many people who live in other rich countries are appalled when they hear about how the American health care system works!

*Drug prices are higher in the United States because the pharmaceutical industry spends billions of dollars on research and development.* It is a fact that American drug companies spend nearly four times as much on sales, administration, and drug advertisement, as they do on the development of drugs. American drug companies do not sell their drugs for such high prices in other rich countries. According to Dr. LeBow, "Their profits as a percent of sales run about 19 percent, compared to a median of about 5 percent for all the Fortune 500 companies." American drug companies claim that the U.S. pharmaceutical industry carries the burden of doing research and development (R&D) for the rest of the world. This claim cannot be taken seriously, as the rich countries of Europe (combined) put out approximately the same number of new drugs a year as the American drug companies. The pharmaceutical industry in America also gets huge taxpayer subsidies from government-supported drug research done by the National Institutes of Health and American universities.

*Universal health care can be achieved through incremental or piecemeal change.* This has been the mantra of many policy makers and legislators in the United States, but following this approach has created a more fragmented and bureaucratic health care system. Each new entitlement program enacted creates new 'eligibility factors,' as well as further administrative costs. The price of health insurance and prescription drugs will continue to rise at a rate of at least twice that of inflation for the near future. The price of health insurance and prescription drugs will continue to rise at a rate of at least twice that of inflation for the near future. With these ever-increasing costs, a growing number of uninsured and underinsured, the shifting by corporate America of more health care costs to their employees, and a diminishing ability to fund state and federal financed safety net programs like Medicaid; there is a definitive need for a comprehensive solution to insure all of the people in the United States. An incremental approach to health care has simply not worked! As David Broder said in an op-ed piece in the *Washington Post*, "It is … clear that tinkering around the edges cannot, for long, withstand the adverse trends that are at work, let alone reverse them."

*Immigrants (legal or illegal) are crowding emergency rooms thus increasing the cost of health care for everyone in America.* There is no data to justify such a statement, except possibly, to a certain extent, in states on the southern border of the United States. Common sense suggests that an overwhelming number of immigrants are usually young and less likely to fall ill than the native born, hence they are less likely to use ER facilities. Illegal immigrants do contribute to the U.S economy in the form of paying taxes, and many contribute money to Social Security that they may never receive back. Reports quote New York Mayor, Michael Bloomberg, as saying that the New York City economy would suffer a severe jolt if any efforts were made to deport illegal immigrants already in the United States. A recent study suggested that immigrants have an average life span that is two years longer than that of native-born Americans. Thus, blaming the cost of health care on immigrants is another myth propagated by some politicians and media people for their personal gain or ratings.

## The cost of competition

Arnold S. Relman, MD, wrote in the *New England Journal of Medicine*, August 30, 2001, that "In all parts of the healthcare system, the providers of care see themselves as competing businesses struggling to survive in a hostile economic climate, and they act accordingly. The predictable result is a fragmented, inefficient, and expensive system."

Up to 25 or 30% of health care dollars are wasted on unnecessary tests, unproven or unwanted procedures, overpriced drugs, new devices that are no better than the cheaper products they replaced, unwanted and hyped drug advertisements, and the administrative cost of managing a fragmented health care system. This is a fact well documented by professionals who have looked into the rising cost of health care.

Maggie Mahar wrote an excellent book called *Money-Driven Medicine.* Her explanation of the laws of supply and demand as they pertain to the health care industry is nicely summed up on the flaps of the hardcopy version of her book:

> In theory, free market competition should tame health care inflation. In fact, Mahar demonstrates, when it comes to medicine, the traditional laws of supply and demand do not apply. Normally, when supply expands, prices fall. But in the health care industry, as the number and variety of drugs, devices and treatments multiplies, demand rises to absorb the excess, and prices climb. Meanwhile, the perverse incentives of a fee-for-service system reward health care providers for doing more, not less.

To this can be added the 'fear factor' of the uninsured and underinsured; they put off the treatment of their ailments or medical conditions until a much later stage. This must contribute to added costs in the health care system, because it prevents such patients from seeking help early, before an ailment or medical condition becomes an acute case.

There is a kind of scramble for dollars by every interested party in the health care industry, which has proven extraordinarily expensive in terms of the quality of care, and in terms of cost. In general, most policy makers, and especially legislators, have further accentuated the problem of not resolving a comprehensive, cost effective health care system, because either they allow dogmatized ideologies to cloud their vision, or they allow lobbyists who contribute heavily to their political power to tie their hands.

Maggie Mahar states in her book,

> The result is a Hobbesian marketplace where a war of 'all against all' pits the health care industry's players against one another: hospital vs. hospital, doctor vs. hospital, doctor vs. doctor,

hospital vs. insurer, insurer vs. hospital, insurer vs. insurer, insurer vs. drug maker, drugmaker vs. drugmaker. In this adversarial environment, "competitors do not create value, they divide it. And sometimes, they destroy it," says Michael Porter, a Harvard Business School professor well known for his writings on market competition.

To this statement, we can add the fact that lawyers who bring frivolous lawsuits and malpractice cases, and who actively take legal positions with one side or the other, further accentuate problems in the current health care system.

What are the solutions to the issues discussed above? The following chapter looks at different approaches to health care reform.

# CHAPTER VI

# Different Approaches to Health Care Reform

## Secretary George Shultz's approach to health care reform

When George Schultz gave a lecture on health care reform at the famous Salk Institute in San Diego on July 23, 2008, I had the opportunity to attend his lecture and to ask him questions later. Soon after, I read his book titled *A Guide to Social Security & Health Care Reform*, in which he and co-author John B. Shoven provide guidelines to reform the American health care system.

They write, "There is a growing conviction in this country that everyone should have the opportunity for access to the health care system. Our proposals would give everyone the opportunity to have access to the health care system in an organized way." Their approach to health care is based on the 'private system', which is more money-driven, offers more competition and more choice in insurance, and includes Health Savings Accounts (HSAs) in order to cut down on costs. The Shultz-Shoven Health initiatives would:

- Encourage national, rather than state, markets in health insurance—according to them, this promotes competition and choice, which puts downward pressure on costs.

- Promote enhanced consumer information about health services and quality—medical records on the quality of hospitals, health service providers, and the effectiveness of alternative treatments should be made public, while the privacy of individuals should be protected.

- Strengthen the incentives for company-sponsored Health Savings Accounts (HSAs) and accompanying catastrophic insurance—by making them portable across employers while permitting tax-deductible health spending for those who have fully participated in an HSA program.

▪ Make tax-deductible HSAs and relatively low-cost catastrophic insurance available to all those who do not have employer-sponsored plans.

Their main suggestion for Medicare and Medicaid is to provide risk-adjusted vouchers. They suggest that in order to contain costs in health spending, in particular with Medicare and Medicaid, it is necessary to transform benefits from services to money. Money could take the form of medical vouchers. People would then have a choice in how that money is spent. For example, some might choose to buy comprehensive insurance, and some might opt to cover only certain conditions, while others might opt for general medical insurance plus HSAs. Vouchers, they say, would allow the government to gain more control over the growth in spending because an established amount of health care buying power would replace an open-ended entitlement to services.

Schultz writes, "The era in which the government can promise Americans access to every medical treatment that might work cannot last. This is not radical thinking; everything else in the economy is rationed today by the market system, the best rationing system ever developed. People acquire what they want, limited by what they can afford. The same logic will apply to health care. Americans will have the health care system they want and will choose the services most valuable to them, but they must be limited by what they can afford." Competition among providers of the various forms of health insurance is also an essential element of the Shultz-Shoven health care plan.

**Senator McCain's Health System Reform**

McCain's 'Health System Reform' is built upon the following four pillars, as described in his campaign:

*Affordability:* The care is more affordable for all Americans, which ensures that drug companies, doctors, insurance companies, hospitals, and every aspect of the health care system compete vigorously to respond to the needs of the people. It rewards quality, promotes prevention, and delivers health care more effectively and efficiently, which ensures that everybody can afford his or her choice of health care.

*Access & Choice:* Every American should have access to affordable, quality coverage of his or her choice, including the choice to keep existing coverage, not only coverage chosen by government bureaucrats or insurance companies.

*Portability & Security:* Everybody should be allowed to keep his or her health insurance as they move from job to job or home to home. It also means protecting every American's security from unforeseen health events by expanding coverage and savings options.

*Quality:* John McCain believes in strengthening health care quality by promoting research and development of new treatment models such as wellness, investing in technology, and empowering Americans with better information on quality.

McCain's vision is that health care should be available to all and not limited by where you work or how much you make. Families should be in charge of their health care dollars and have more control over care. Families should be able to purchase health insurance nationwide, and across state lines. John McCain's plan would reform the tax code to offer more choices beyond employer-based health insurance coverage. Families would have the option of keeping employer-based health insurance or they could receive a direct refundable tax credit—effectively cash—of $2,500 for individuals and $5,000 for families to offset the cost of insurance. McCain's plan would encourage and expand the benefits of HSAs for families, an important step in the direction of putting families in charge of what they pay for.

*Ensuring care for higher risk patients and the uninsured*

McCain recognized that it is difficult for patients with pre-existing conditions to get health insurance. He suggested working with governors to develop a best practice model that states could follow—a Guaranteed Access Plan (GAP). One approach would establish a nonprofit corporation that would contract with insurers to cover patients who have been denied insurance, and could join with other state plans to enlarge pools and lower overhead costs. There would be reasonable limits on premiums, and assistance would be available for Americans below a certain income level. He planned to work with Congress, the governors, and industry, to make sure this approach was fully funded.

### *Lowering health care costs*

McCain suggested a number of issues in lowering the cost of health care, most of which are listed below:

- Drug prices can be lowered by the safe re-importation of drugs from countries like Canada, and by the faster introduction of generic drugs.

- Costs can be reduced by emphasizing prevention, early intervention, healthy habits, new treatment models, new public health infrastructure, and the use of information technology.

- Government should promote greater access to walk-in clinics in retail outlets.

- The Medicaid and Medicare payment system should be reformed so that these entitlement programs do not pay for preventable medical errors or mismanagement.

- Congress should pass laws to eliminate lawsuits directed at doctors who followed clinical guidelines and adhered to safety protocols.

- Transparency should be brought to health care costs wherein the public is informed on treatment options and doctors' records, and transparency should be required regarding medical outcomes, quality of care, costs, and prices.

## Critical comments on the Shultz-Shoven and McCain Reform Proposals

Both health care plans are fundamentally flawed, as these plans would lead neither to universal health care reform nor to a cost-efficient and effective health care system in America.

The Shultz-Shoven health initiatives are primarily market driven, with more competition and more health insurance plans, but without any basic structural changes. These initiatives are unworkable. To say, "Americans will have the health care system they want and will choose the services most valuable to them, but they must be limited by what they can afford," is not being realistic.

These initiatives would lead to more people without basic health insurance and people would be at the mercy of insurance companies and the escalating cost of drugs, benefiting only those two industries.

Shultz also wrote that "An essential step toward containing health spending, particularly in Medicare and Medicaid, is to transform benefits from services to money." Shultz-Shoven suggested in their book some kind of risk-adjusted voucher system for Medicare, Medicaid, and HSA accounts. Their whole range of suggestions would further lead to money driven medicine, which is principally based on the ability to afford health care. For these reasons, if nothing else, the Schultz-Shoven plan would be untenable. They have also overlooked major problems and issues, as mentioned earlier.

McCain's vision of reforming the health system is not as radical as that of Shultz, but he too supported the idea of further competition by introducing insurance policies across state lines and promoting Health Savings Accounts. His system reform is only a piece-meal incremental solution, which does not address the issues of 47 million uninsured people. Some of the points he mentioned are vague and would be difficult to implement. He advocated tax credits of $2,500 for singles and $5,000 for married couples, but the average cost of health care coverage is nearly $12,000 for a family of four at this time.

*Most people have difficulty understanding one insurance policy with co-payments and deductibles—how then are people supposed to understand hundreds of policies written by lawyers? It is simply not practical.*

There are a few good points in McCain's proposal in terms of reducing the cost of health care, but he did not suggest a detailed and practical reform that would be workable and cover the whole population of America. He avoided problems related to insurance and drug companies, and the problem of how to achieve a unified and comprehensive reform that also dealt with the fragmented state of the current American system.

*Finally, health care reform cannot be left to market forces without regulating insurance and drug companies. We should learn lessons from the near collapse of the financial system in 2008–09 when markets failed to self regulate. Common sense, ethics, and wisdom, were put aside, as the sole motivation was greed and selfishness.*

Massachusetts and California were the first states in America in which both the state Assembly and the state Senate passed universal health care bills in 2006. Below, the universal health systems of both states are briefly summarized.

**Massachusetts Health Care Reform Plan**

Full implementation of the plan came into effect on July 1, 2007. Massachusetts enjoys a strong foundation of employer sponsored insurance, and is also supported by expansive Medicare and Medicaid entitlement programs, making it easier to achieve universal health care coverage. Only 10% of the population was uninsured at the time, compared to the national average of over 16%.

The Massachusetts Health Care Reform plan mandated that everyone in the state purchase health insurance by July 1, 2007. The bill imposed financial penalties of up to 50% of the cost of a health insurance plan on those who did not comply—this was done via income tax filings. The plan requires the participation of both individuals and companies, and includes a requirement that employers with more than ten employees either provide health insurance coverage, or pay a 'fair share' contribution of up to $295 annually, per employee, to the Commonwealth Care Trust Fund.

*Insurance market reforms:* These are an important component of the plan, which merges the individual and small-group insurance markets, and are expected to reduce premium costs for individuals by up to 24%.

*Government-funded subsidies:* Another central piece of the plan is that government-funded subsidies are provided to low-income individuals in order to purchase health insurance. The Massachusetts Health Insurance program provides sliding-scale subsidies to individuals with incomes up to 300% of the federal poverty level, for the purchase of health insurance. Individuals with income less than 100% of the federal poverty level are not required to pay any premiums.

*Medicaid expanded:* The plan includes an expansion of Medicaid to children and covers 92,500 younger citizens.

*Preservation of the safety net:* A new Safety Net Care fund that includes the Free Care Pool and other Medicaid funds replaced the existing Free Care Pool that reimbursed providers of health care for uncompensated care. A new fee schedule for standardizing health care provider reimbursements is included. The funds now go into a health insurance subsidy program as the uninsured gained coverage and uncompensated care costs dropped. The plan also created an Essential Community Provider grant program to support safety net hospitals and community health centers.

Plan financing, expected to cost $1.2 billion over three years, relies on the redistribution of existing funding, which includes federal Medicaid payments previously paid to safety net providers, and state funds from the Free Care Pool.

**Key questions about the Massachusetts Plan and its deficiencies**

The objective of the plan is to provide health care coverage for every resident of Massachusetts, which is laudable as it is the first state in the United States to provide universal care. But it leaves many unanswered questions. Key questions are:

- Will insurance companies offer health care plans that are affordable?

- Will employers maintain or expand coverage?

- Is the plan adequately funded in an era when health costs are steadily rising?

There is nothing in the plan that adequately addresses how to cut, seriously, the general costs of the health care system, which spends over 16% of the nation's GDP. Nor does it deal with issues raised in the previous chapter. The main deficiencies of the plan are:

- There is no funding for preventive measures included in the plan for promoting healthy living styles in order to cut down on illnesses and diseases. Substantial funding is needed for advertising campaigns to educate people on this subject.

- There are too many fragmented federal and state entitlement programs, leading to excessive paperwork and bureaucracy. It is estimated that over 25% of health budgets are spent in administering these programs. Costs must be cut by combining and simplifying these entitlement programs.

- There is no provision for use of electronic medical cards essential for cutting down the cost of health care.

The Massachusetts plan represents a unique approach to expanding health care coverage for all. It provides residents with health care regardless of income. It protects them from having to declare bankruptcy when the cost of medical care becomes excessive, as was true in the past. Its main drawback is that it may not be able to cover rising health care costs in the future.

This plan can at least influence federal and other state governments to start debating on how to come up with a cost effective health care system that covers every resident in the United States.

## California's universal health care bill SB 840

California Health Insurance Reliability Act, SB 840 (Kuehl) was passed by both the state Senate and the state Assembly; however, Governor Schwarzenegger returned the bill without signature in September 2006. It covered all state residents, including undocumented residents, Californians traveling out of state for up to ninety days, and California retirees living out of state if they paid the required taxes to the Health Care Fund.

*Funding:* All federal, state, and county monies spent on health care would be reallocated to the state Health Care Fund. This would supply about one-third of the needed funding. The remaining funds would come from state health taxes that would replace health insurance premiums now paid to insurance companies, and co-pays and deductibles being paid to health providers. Premiums would be based upon what individuals and families pay in proportion to their income, and what employers pay in proportion to wages. Basically, it would be a single-payer health care system very similar to the health care systems of Scandinavian countries.

*Structure and Administration:* A Health Care Commissioner would be elected every eight years with a two-term limit. The Commissioner would supervise the California Health Insurance Agency that administers the California Health Insurance System. The Commissioner would appoint the Deputy Health Care Commissioner, the Health Insurance Fund Director, the Consumer Advocate, the Chief Medical Officer, the Director of Health Planning, the Director of Partnerships for Health, the Director of Payments Board, and regional Health Planning directors. All the designated officials would have designated responsibilities within the health care system.

*Regional health care centers:* The Commissioner would establish ten of them that would be headed by Regional Health Planning directors. Funding would be established by the Commissioner for each region, and it would support local decision making in the health-planning message. Patients would be able to receive care in more than one region.

Umang Malhotra

*Health Insurance Policy Board:* This would be chaired by the Commissioner and it would include the seven appointed state officers, the state public health officer, and two representatives from the regional planning boards. A Public Advisory Committee to advise the board, representing doctors, nurses, hospitals, dentists, health practitioners, pharmacists, mental health providers, consumers, businesses, and labor would be appointed by the Assembly, the Senate, and the governor. The Health Insurance Policy Board:

- Establishes the scope of services

- Sets priorities and guidelines for evaluations, research, capital investment, and public input

- Determines the need for change or increase in health insurance premiums

*Inspector General of the California Health Care system:* A position of Inspector General would be established in the office of the Attorney General, and would be appointed by the governor. The Inspector General would have authority to investigate fraud or misconduct by employees of the Health Care Agency, providers, or consumers.

*Partnership for Health:* Would establish collaboration between the California Health Insurance Agency and each region, by way of the Consumer Advocate, the Chief Medical Officer, and regional advocates and directors. Each Partnership for Health would support health maintenance, disease prevention, good communication between patients and providers, health education and better quality of care.

*Transition:* A transition Commissioner of Health Insurance, appointed by the governor with Senate confirmation, would serve until the first election. The transition Commissioner would initiate the establishment of the health care system in every aspect, with assistance from a transition advisory group.

*Benefits and exclusions:* Included are inpatient and outpatient services, physicians and licensed health care professionals, diagnostic imaging, laboratory services, emergency care, rehabilitative care, preventive care, mental health care, emergency or necessary transportation, prescription drugs, immunizations, blood products, health education, hospice care, dialysis, and up to 100 days in a skilled nursing facility. Dentistry, vision care, podiatry, chiropractics, acupuncture, religious healing protected under federal or state statues, adult day care, case management, substance abuse treatment, language interpretation, and durable medical equipment, including prosthetics, eyeglasses and hearing aids, are also covered. The Commissioner could add benefits above those required by the bill, if the budget permitted.

Cosmetic procedures, private hospital rooms with no medical necessity, care by unlicensed providers, and procedures or medications with no proven medical value, are all excluded. The Chief Medical Officer could authorize treatment not included in the benefit package.

*Budget and Capital Expenditure:* The annual budget would be prepared by the Commissioner, including facility and provider budgets for both fee-for-service and integrated systems (capitated budgets), purchasing, research and innovation, and workforce development.

*Capital improvements to health care facilities:* These would be in accordance with plans made by the Commissioner and regional directors. All capital investments including facility improvements, land and office space purchases, and large medical equipment purchases, would be subject to the capital planning guidelines. The Commissioner would establish standards for small capital expenditures funded through operating budgets. Capital improvements would minimize unneeded expansion of facilities and services, and would correct health care disparities. The system would not pay for mandatory earthquake retrofits.

*Research:* This would include studies to improve quality of health care, administration of the system, communication amongst health care providers, and education of patients.

*Cost containment:* The Commissioner and regional directors would be responsible for keeping overall costs within the budget. The bill mandates that spending grow no faster than the average growth of the state GDP and of the population. Regional and statewide cost containment methods are listed in detail in the bill.

The Commissioner may ask the legislature for an increase in health care taxes, when and if cost control measures are insufficient.

SB 840 is a comprehensive, single-payer system. It was introduced by Democratic California State Senator Sheila Kuehl, Chair of the Health Committee, and was passed by the California Senate. It has many similarities to Scandinavian health care systems, which are considered some of the best in the world, and which have health care costs 40–50% less, as a percentage of GDP, than American costs. Although Senator Kuehl's term ended, the campaign continues with SB 840's reintroduction by Democratic California State Senator Mark Leno, now known as SB 810 (Leno).

**Critical comments on California's universal health care bill**

SB 840 would remove widespread anxiety amongst the uninsured and under-insured residents of California in case of illness or disease. It would encourage people either to see a doctor for either preventive care, or consult a doctor immediately if they notice any symptoms of illness. Furthermore, it would also be of comfort to those residents who otherwise would have to declare bankruptcy when unable to pay medical bills following an unforeseen accident or extended illness.

In my view, including the VA budget into the State Health Care Fund further reduces the cost of health care and makes a stronger bill. VA hospitals should also become integrated parts of the whole health care system, with an internal market created between hospitals, to provide the best health care, in a cost effective manner, for the patients. In this way, excess resources for treatment or operations can shift between facilities, according to the needs and requirements of patients.

It is also imperative that the state spend money to promote healthy living choices and to educate people in taking preventive measures, like regular physical check ups, especially for those over forty years old.

In addition, the bill would advance the idea of an electronic health care card for each resident, tied into an information technology system, to cut down medical mistakes and reduce costs. The effective use of information technology to reduce administrative costs is a vital part of any workable solution the health care crisis. This system would be cost-efficient, as it would eliminate much of the paperwork.

The California Health Insurance Reliability Act, SB 840, and the Massachusetts Health Care Reform Plan, are two ways to create universal health care. Another way would be to create a universal system that has services similar to those mentioned under "*Benefits*" in SB 840, plus top-up insurance, which could include extra benefits, as required by the patient. This would cover emergencies and contingencies, such as waiting lists that might develop for a particular operation or procedure. Each state could follow one of the universal health care plans mentioned.

**The Schwarzenegger-Nuñez Plan for California**

Republican Governor Arnold Schwarzenegger and Democratic California Assembly Speaker Fabian Nuñez (Los Angeles) reached a tentative agreement on December 14, 2007, for a $14 billion plan to overhaul California's health care system. Under this health plan ABX1 1, nearly all residents would be required to obtain health coverage, including nearly 3.6 million uninsured Californians. The plan was passed by the California Assembly but died in the Senate Health Committee, which blocked the plan by a seven to one majority. Hence, this plan did not come to a vote on the floor of the full Senate.

The plan provided tax credits to the following groups for purchasing coverage:

- California residents who spend more than 5.5% of their income on health insurance if their income does not exceed 400% of the federal poverty level

- Residents who spend more than 10% of their income on health insurance if their income does not exceed 700% of the poverty level

Low-income residents and undocumented immigrants would be exempt from the coverage mandate if coverage would require them to spend more than 5% of their income on minimal coverage, and providing also that they did not qualify for public health care programs. The plan also would extend coverage to children whose family's income did not exceed 300% of the poverty level, regardless of immigration status.

Funding for the plan would have come from employers' contributions, and taxation. Employers' contributions would be adjusted to a new sliding scale for businesses with payrolls as follows:

- Up to $250,000 would contribute 1% of payroll towards coverage

- From $250,000 to $1 million would contribute 4% toward coverage

- From $1 million to $15 million would contribute 6%

- Above $15 would contribute 6.5%

Some other funding envisaged in the Schwarzenegger-Nuñez plan:

- A 4% tax on hospital revenue in an effort to secure matching federal funds and boost Medicaid reimbursements for services

- About $5 billion in anticipated new federal funding, including Medi-Cal (Note: Medi-Cal is California's Medicaid program.)

Schwarzenegger agreed with Nuñez to finance health care reform partially by raising the state's tobacco tax, even though tobacco companies spent more than $60 million to help defeat a proposed tobacco tax increase the year before. Earlier the governor had favored a lease of California's lottery.

## Flaws in the Schwarzenegger-Nuñez Health Care Plan

In California, many grassroots organizations are pushing for a single-payer universal health care system. The Schwarzenegger-Nuñez Health Care Plan ABX1 1 has many flaws. It is not universal, and it relies on the policy choices of insurance companies. The plan would neither control health care costs nor bring major reform to the problems and issues involving insurance companies that the current health care system has. For this reason, it was voted down in the California Senate Health Care Committee.

Senators Tom Daschle, Hillary Clinton, and Barack Obama all proposed health care plans in 2008. Following is a look at their plans.

### Senator Tom Daschle's health care proposals

Daschle has been a keen observer of the history of health care reform and has been involved in bringing about changes. He writes in his book entitled, *What We Can Do About the Health-Care Crisis,* that over 47 million people are uninsured and an additional 16 million are under-insured. He calls this stunning and shameful for the richest country in the world. The United States is the only industrialized nation that does not guarantee necessary health care to its people.

From the years 2000 to 2007 U.S. health insurance premiums rose 98%, while wages increased by only 23%, according to Senator Daschle. He believes the problem is rooted in the complexity of the health care issue and in the power of interest groups—doctors, hospitals, insurers, drug companies, researchers, patient advocates—all of whom have a financial dependence on the system. In his book he writes, "More troubling is the idea that some doctors order tests, perform procedures, and prescribe drugs, because they have a financial stake in doing so." He also recognizes a fragmented and uncoordinated health care system, which gives purchasers of insurance little power to negotiate for lower prices, as well as the waste of system resources on paperwork and administrative costs. In 2003, a study published in the *New England Journal of Medicine* by three Harvard researchers concluded that 31% of every dollar spent on health care in the U.S. is consumed by administrative costs. Daschle says this survey suggests that American health care providers spend one-third to one-half of their time in completing paperwork. Compared to the most efficient nations (France, Finland, and Japan), American administrative costs are three times higher per dollar of health care spending.

He also notes that a New York Times/CBS News poll conducted in February 2007 found that a majority of Americans wanted the federal government to guarantee health insurance to every citizen. More than 60% of the respondents said they would be willing to pay more in taxes to ensure that everybody is covered. Most people in America agree that a reformed health care system must focus on access, affordability, and quality.

*Options for Coverage*

Most of the world's highest-ranking health care systems employ some kind of single-payer system. According to Daschle, a single-payer system is problematic in the U.S. Polls show that seniors are happier with Medicare and younger people with private insurance. Opponents of reform have demonized a government-run system as socialized medicine.

Daschle asks, "If the passage of a single-payer system is not realistic, what should we do?" Conservatives argue for more choice in insurance, and for allowing out of state insurance companies to compete in other states, but Daschle suggests another alternative, which is to strengthen the employer-based health care system. Employers who do not offer health insurance to employees would have to contribute to a group-rate fund. Employers who offer coverage through this fund would have to offer group-rate insurance to all employees. Supporters of such an 'employer mandate' say it would result in coverage for nearly everyone, since 80% of the uninsured are attached to the work force. They believe that Medicare, Medicaid, and other entitlement programs must be strengthened. Medicaid already serves approximately 50 million people, which surpasses Medicare.

*Federal Health Board (FHB)*

Daschle suggests a Federal Health Board (FHB) along the lines of the Securities and Exchange Commission (SEC), which regulates financial markets. He believes the FHB would have the knowledge to make complicated medical decisions and the independence to resist political pressures.

*Structure and Functions*

The FHB would be a quasi-governmental organization. It would have a Board of Governors consisting of clinicians, health benefit managers, economists, researchers, and other respected experts. The President would appoint the board, which would be confirmed by the Senate. Regional boards would have input from the community and business representatives in their areas. These boards would coordinate policies and decisions with the central FHB. The FHB's responsibilities would embrace the following areas:

- It would set rules for an expanded Federal Employee Health Benefits Program (FEHBP), placing conditions on private insurers wishing to participate, and develop guidelines for premiums and marketing practices.

- It would develop policies to prevent insurers from shunning high-cost enrollees.

- It would give guidance to maintain choice in insurance, reduce administrative costs, promote good insurer practices, and protect consumers.

- It would promote 'high-value medical care' by recommending coverage for those drugs and procedures backed by solid evidence, and it would exert influence by ranking services and therapies by their health and cost impacts.

- It would promote prevention.

- It would promote electronic health records in the Veterans Administration, Medicare, Medicaid and other entitlement programs, and for the general public.

- It would make decisions by soliciting public comments, and it would promote transparency.

- It would align incentives with high-quality care through direct-to-consumers advertising, preventing drug companies from ramping up patient demand for new drugs that are no better than older, cheaper alternatives.

- The FHB also might play a role in rationalizing health care infrastructure and dealing with the current fragmented system.

Finally, Daschle suggests increasing the number of community health centers and government-funded clinics that provide basic care to the poor and uninsured. He also proposes setting up a single standard of care and coverage in all these programs, which would be a model for every other provider and payer.

*Enforcement*

Daschle says the FHB would not be regulatory, but that its recommendations would have teeth because all federal health programs would have to abide by them, and those programs account for nearly 40% of all health spending. It makes sense to create one set of policies for all federally funded health programs. Daschle finds it hard to believe that insurers participating in the new FEHBP would find it difficult to maintain separate sets of rules for enrollees inside and outside the pool.

**Critical comments about Daschle's health care proposals**

The FHB would only solve one part of the nation's health-care crisis. Any comprehensive reform plan must also provide affordable coverage to all Americans. To do so, responsibility must be shared. Congress would need to create a framework for financing health care coverage, and the executive branch would have to implement key elements of the reform plan, such as promoting IT infrastructure.

The SEC is not the best comparison for this idea. It did a very bad job of regulating financial markets in late 2008, especially in the case of the scandal involving former NASDAQ chairman Bernie Madoff, whose company ran Ponzi schemes, losing nearly $50 billion of clients' money despite red flags that were raised over a period of ten years. The FHB would need to have much better oversight.

Senator Daschle has a series of good proposals for providing universal health care in the U.S., and most of them could be applied as an interim measure, but they would not bring down the cost of health care. Strict rules would have to be set for insurance and drug companies as well. The government must also consider how to limit frivolous lawsuits and how to prevent lobbyists and interest groups from having undue influence on the formulation of health care proposals.

## Senator Clinton's Universal Health Care Choices plan

As a Senator, Hillary Clinton unveiled her universal health care plan during her campaign for presidential nominee of the Democratic Party in 2008. She repeatedly stated that universal health care was the most passionate and urgent issue for her to handle if she became President of the United States. During her campaign, she said that the economy and health care were the key domestic issues she encountered from the electorate in the U.S. Her universal health care plan is very similar to that of Senator Edwards, and nearly 95% the same as the one of Senator Obama. She preferred a single-payer system, which she recognized would be very difficult to get through Congress.

Senator Clinton estimated that her plan would cost an additional sum of about $120 billion a year to implement in the U.S., and said she would deliver a universal health care system for Americans within her first term as President. The cost would be covered by revoking President Bush's tax cuts for the wealthiest Americans earning more than $250,000 per year. This tax cut for the rich expires in 2010 if an extension is not approved by Congress. She also proposed taking away tax incentives given to the oil companies during the Bush Presidency —considering that oil companies already enjoy huge profits—Exxon alone made over $40 billion in profits in the year 2007. Below are the major points of Senator Clinton's health care plan:

*Offer New Coverage for the Insured and Uninsured*

Key criteria of Senator Clinton's health care plan were:

- Require the health care plan to be mandatory, and to cover the more than 47 million uninsured people as well as tens of millions more at risk of losing coverage.

- the same choice of health plan options as Members of Congress receive.

- Guarantee the quality of health care to be as good as the typical plan offered to Members of Congress, which usually includes both mental health and dental coverage.

Clinton pointed out that Americans who are satisfied with the coverage they have could keep it, or choose from new health care plans with quality care and lower premiums.

*Lower Premiums, Increase Security, and Promote Shared Responsibility*

- Reducing Costs: By removing hidden taxes, stressing prevention, and focusing on efficiency and modernization, the plan would improve quality and lower costs.

- Strengthening Security: The plan would ensure that job loss or family illnesses would never lead to a loss of coverage or to exorbitant costs.

- Ending Unfair Health Insurance Discrimination: By creating a level-playing field of insurance rules across states and markets, the plan would ensure that no American was denied coverage, refused renewal, unfairly priced out of the market, or forced to pay excessive insurance company premiums.

- Insurance and Drug Companies: Insurance companies would end discrimination based on pre-existing conditions or expectations of illness, and ensure high value for every premium dollar. Drug companies would provide accurate information and offer fair prices on drugs.

- Individuals: would be required to get and keep insurance in a system where insurance was affordable and accessible.

- Providers: would work collaboratively with patients and businesses to deliver high quality, affordable care.

- Employers: would help finance the system; large employers would be expected to provide health insurance or contribute to the cost of coverage; small businesses would receive a tax credit to continue, or begin to offer coverage.

- Government: would ensure that health insurance is always affordable and never a crushing burden on any family. It would implement reforms to improve quality and lower cost.

*Ensure Affordable Coverage for All*

Senator Clinton's health care plan would:

- Provide working families with a tax credit.

- Limit insurance premium payments to a percentage of an individual's or family's income.

- Create a new small business tax credit. A new health care tax credit for small businesses will provide an incentive for job-based coverage.

- Strengthen Medicaid and SCHIP programs for the most vulnerable populations.

- Launch a health legacy initiative for retirees: a new tax credit for qualifying private and public retiree health plans would offset a significant portion of catastrophic accident or illness expenditures.

## Senator Barack Obama's plan

Senator Barack Obama announced his "Plan for a Healthy America" during a speech in Iowa City on May 29, 2007. A brief extract from his speech is quoted below.

> We now face an opportunity—and an obligation—to turn the page on the failed politics of yesterday's health care debates... My plan begins by covering every American. If you already have health insurance, the only thing that will change for you under this plan is the amount of money you will spend on premiums. That will be less. If you are one of the 47 million Americans who do not have health insurance, you will have it after this plan becomes law. No one will be turned away because of a preexisting condition or illness.

Senator Obama clearly stated that the main reason that millions of Americans are uninsured or underinsured is rising medical costs. The 47 million uninsured Americans include 9 million children, and there is no sign of slowing in the trend of escalating costs. He stated that health care costs are skyrocketing, and health insurance premiums have risen four times faster than wages over the past six years.

Obama's health care plan stressed that too little is spent on prevention and public health—the nation faces epidemics of obesity and chronic disease, as well as the new threats of pandemic flu and bioterrorism. He stated that less than four cents of every health care dollar is being spent on prevention and public health.

Obama's plan would make available to all Americans a new national health plan, which would include the self-employed and small businesses. It would enable them to buy affordable health coverage similar to the plan available to Members of Congress.

This health care plan would not be mandatory, but it would require that all children be insured. It would also give young adults more options by allowing them to be insured under their parents' policies up to the age of twenty-five. It is estimated that the Obama health care plan would cost about $60 billion yearly. The cost would also be paid for by revoking President Bush's tax cuts for the wealthiest Americans, those earning over $250,000 per year. He would take away tax incentives given to the oil companies during the Bush Presidency as well. He predicted that his health care plan would become law before the end of his first term as President. The Obama plan would have the following features:

- *Guaranteed eligibility:* No American would be turned away from any insurance plan because of illness or pre-existing conditions.

- *Comprehensive benefits:* The benefits package would be similar to that offered through Federal Employees Health Benefits Program (FEHBP), which covers members of Congress.

- *Affordable*: Premiums, co-pays, and deductibles would be brought under control.

- *Subsidies:* Individuals and families who do not qualify for Medicaid or SCHIP, but who need assistance, would receive an income-related federal subsidy to buy into the new public plan or purchase a private health care plan.

- *Simplified paperwork and health care plans:* Simplification would help to reduce costs.

- *Easy enrollment:* The new public plan would be simple to enroll in and provide ready access to coverage.

- *Portability and choice:* Participants in the new public plan and the National Health Insurance Exchange would be able to move from job to job without changing or jeopardizing their health care coverage.

- *Quality and efficiency:* Participating insurance companies in the new public program would be required to report data to ensure that standards for quality, health information technology, and administration are being met.

In order to achieve the goals of his health care plan, once the plan was signed into law, Obama said he would implement the following points:

- *A National Health Insurance Exchange:* would be created to help individuals who wish to purchase a private insurance plan. The exchange would act as a watchdog group and help to reform the private insurance market. It would create rules and standards for participating insurance plans, to ensure fairness, and to make individual coverage more affordable and accessible. The exchange would require that all the plans offered are at least as generous as the new public plan, and have the same standards for quality and efficiency.

- *Employer contribution:* Employers that do not offer or make a meaningful contribution to the cost of quality health coverage for their employees would be required to contribute a percentage of payroll tax toward the costs of the national plan. Small employers that meet certain revenue thresholds would be exempt.

- *Mandatory coverage of children:* The plan would require that all children have health care coverage and would allow young adults up to the age of twenty-five years to have coverage through their parents' plans.

- *Expansion of Medicaid and SCHIP:* Eligibility for Medicaid and SCHIP programs would be expanded and the plan would ensure that these programs continued to serve their critical safety net function. (Note: An extension of the SCHIP program, which expanded coverage to more children and to pregnant women, was passed into law on February 4, 2009, two weeks after Obama was sworn in as President.)

- *Flexibility for State Plans:* The plan would build on the health care plans of individual states wherever they have acted. Each state could continue with their own plan, providing they met the minimum standards of the national plan.

Senator Obama promised to lower health care costs by modernizing the U.S. health care system. The plan would also reimburse employer health care plans for a portion of the catastrophic costs they incur above a threshold, if they guarantee such savings are used to reduce the cost of workers' premiums.

Health care reform is a key priority of the Obama administration since he became President in January of 2009.

## Some discussion on, and solutions for, the Clinton and Obama plans

The health care plans presented by Senators Clinton and Obama have basic flaws in controlling the cost of premiums and drugs. It would be almost impossible to control the cost of health care without control of lobbying, a major overhaul of insurance companies, the ability of the government to negotiate drug prices by the State, and some form of legislation to contain malpractice insurance and frivolous medical lawsuits. Senator John Edwards repeatedly warned that no universal health care system would be feasible and cost effective without curbing the power of lobbyists who promote insurance and drug companies' interests to politicians, while at the same time making huge campaign contributions to the politicians that advocate for universal health care.

On the one hand, Clinton's universal health care plan would be mandatory but it does not state how the requirement for individuals to buy insurance would be implemented. On the other hand, Obama's plan mandates only that those under the age of twenty-five be covered through their parents' health care plans, but does not cover all adults. This would then leave nearly 15 million people still uninsured under his plan, according to Senator Clinton. Obama argued however, that if insurance premiums were reduced by $2,500 per family per year, then most of the un-insured would sign on. Both plans have built-in insurance coverage for the needy and the poor. It is not clear, from the Clinton and Obama health care plans, what they intend to do with more than 12 million illegal immigrants, and how they should be insured, or otherwise brought into the new health care plans. If these people were not brought into the system, they would be a burden on emergency rooms for treatment, which is expensive. There are also no concrete solutions for how health care would be portable if people moved from one job to another, or crossed state boundaries for their work.

Both Clinton and Obama failed to define clearly how to control rampant insurance premiums, and varying degrees of deductibles and co-payments, by the hundreds of insurance companies. Both plans would negotiate drug prices with pharmaceutical companies on the state and/or federal level in order to cut down ever-increasing drug costs. Neither of the plans specified what they intended to do with prescription drug advertising in the media, which creates an unnecessary demand for certain drugs. Nor do they give solutions to skyrocketing malpractice insurance premiums, or for stopping frivolous medical lawsuits.

Again, aggressive actions are needed to control administrative bureaucracies and paperwork in the health industry, and there has to be efficient use of IT in curbing health care costs. The most important thing is to have a tamper-proof IT medical card for each person in the U.S. Such a card is already in existence in the rich countries of Europe.

Both Clinton and Obama preferred to introduce a single-payer health care system, as in other economically developed countries, but they feared it would not get through Congress because many of the legislators in both houses, especially Republicans, are obsessively against so-called socialized medicine. A single-payer system would certainly eliminate insurance companies as the middleman, and put more decision making for patients in the hands of doctors, instead of in the hands of a bureaucrat sitting hundreds of miles away in an insurance company office. It is commendable that both Obama and Clinton took the first steps toward realizing a universal health care system, because they knew that affordable and quality health care for all is a major issue with the American population.

## Closing comments on the health care plans discussed above

Americans are conditioned, to an extent, to think and believe that everything associated with socialism has negative connotations, but ironically, they have never questioned why their military does not have a socialist connotation when it is funded by taxpayers' money, or why their state funded highways do not carry that association. It is for this reason that California Governor Schwarzenegger did not sign the single-payer health bill SB 840, although both legislative branches in the State of California passed it. He quoted the same fear of socialized medicine, in order to appease the insurance and drug companies, and other interest groups that were opposed to the bill.

Sara Elizabeth Rogers, health consultant to former state senator Sheila Kuehl, wrote an article that appeared in Kuehl's newsletter after the failure of the Schwarzenegger-Nuñez health plan ABX1 1. In it, she said:

> I could not help but notice that, historically, the compromises are forged by the exact same powerful interests every time, working like scavengers randomly picking through the ideas of national health insurance, with little consideration given to whether any "reform" was actually going to improve the health care system for the average American.
>
> In fact, a century of such "health care reform" has brought our health care system to the point where it is deeply fragmented, unimaginably costly, and the least effective system in the entire developed world, at delivering either health, or

care. I can't help but wonder where we might have been in terms of universal health care had proponents not forfeited their goal so fast.

Most striking? The grassroots role that physicians repeatedly played in defeating national health insurance. The American Medical Association functioned as an exceptionally effective grassroots movement that was embedded in every community across the nation. They organized education and lobbying campaigns against universal health care, labeling their efforts as "protecting the public health." They hired PR consultants who admitted that they were attempting to label national health insurance as "socialized medicine" for the simple reason that Americans were opposed to socialism.

The American College of Physicians made history by endorsing the idea of a single-payer health care system for California. The American Medical Students Association became a passionate advocate for it. Many grassroots associations like the California Nurses Association and teachers unions, amongst others, supported it as well. In fact, 500 or so organizations gave it their enthusiastic support. These groups continue their evolution into an effective coalition, working tirelessly to educate and organize Californians on the benefits of universal health care. The State of California has been a trendsetter in many ways for the rest of America. There is no doubt that there will be a universal health care system in California in the near future.

Senator Daschle and Secretary Clinton, along with Senator Kennedy all agree that an effective single-payer health care system with applied IT technology is the best possible solution for cutting costs.

Let then each state, in conjunction with the federal government; devise a universal health care system uniquely suitable to its own circumstances and people, whether it is a single-payer system, one with a mixture of public and private financing, or one that includes top-up insurance. After a period of time, each state can then evaluate which universal health care system is the most cost effective in delivering quality care for its population.

# CHAPTER VII

# Cost Effective Solutions to the American Health Care System

## Recommendations

Consideration of the following points is necessary for a rich and large country like America, or the fifty individual states, to provide decent health care with modern medicine for all its entire population.

- Provide each person with health care.

- Subsidize health care for those who cannot afford it: the elderly, sick, and other vulnerable groups.

- Eliminate fragmented entitlement programs, i.e., Medicare, Medicaid, the Veterans Administration, and others financed and managed by federal and state governments. A universal health care system will substantially cut down the waste and cost involved in running these diverse and fragmented entitlement programs.

- Health care should be based on patient needs rather than ability to pay, but there can be limits on what 'basic health care' is covered. Any person can pay top-up insurance to cover an emergency, waiting list, or any other special requirement that may not be immediately available or is rationed under the 'basic health care' provided.

- The role of private insurance companies must be restricted, with limited policies and deductibles, and insurance companies should not be able to pick and choose their clients.

- Solutions must be found to restrict frivolous lawsuits.

- There should be controls placed on the pricing of prescription drugs, as well as on the aggressive advertising of them by pharmaceutical companies.

- America should learn from some of the best practices in the health care systems of the rich countries of Europe, and of Australia, Canada, and Japan.

- An electronic medical card, which includes the medical history of the patient, should be issued for each person in the United States. This would cut down on medical mistakes and paperwork, substantially reducing the cost of health care.

There are only three possibilities on which a universal health care system can be based.

1. A system that is privately funded

2. A system that is a combination of private and public funding

3. A system that is only publicly funded

Number one is not an option, as the health care system will become money driven, with ever escalating health care costs. The system will become unsustainable in a short period, even in the richest and most capitalistic economy in the world. Hence, numbers two and three are the only options, as long as the health care system is not fragmented and it covers all the population in America.

I am convinced that a cost effective American health care system will evolve as long as politicians and policy makers do not clutter up their search for solutions with their ideologies. They will have to swallow their pride too, and confess that they have repeatedly misled the population by claiming that America has the best health care system in the world. They have to transcend preserving their personal power, suppress their egos, and take a good look at the best practices of the health care systems of the other rich nations. They must do this in order to develop and implement a health care system that provides adequate and quality health care for all people. America has to start with a fresh approach to developing a health care system, one that is superior and more cost effective than existing systems in the world. America has the means to develop a newer and better health care system, from scratch, because it has the finest health institutions and hospitals. It also has brilliant minds and doctors who are wise and ethical, and it has a bureaucracy for processing information already in place. Sadly, despite this, the current health care system has not only become money driven, it has become antiquated as well.

*As a starting point to developing a new, simple, and cost effective health system, the President and Congress could set up a commission of about ten people of integrity and character, who are wise and ethical, and give them a clear mandate, which would include the following points:*

- The health care system must be as simple as possible, cover the whole population of America, and cater to patients needs.

- The commission members should study the health care systems of other rich countries and evaluate the best health care practices amongst them.

- The commission should ask why America spends 40–50% more per person than other rich countries do, and gets much less in return.

- The commission should also study the viability of a health care system that either is publicly and privately funded, or solely publicly funded. Either one of these systems could be applied to the whole United States, or to the individual states.

- The commission should consider an electronic medical card for each resident of the United States, which contains the complete medical history of the person since birth. This electronic card would need the highest standard of security to ensure that only medical professionals dealing with the patient could activate it. Such a card would cut down on medical mistakes as well as on paperwork, thereby reducing costs in the health care system.

- Emphasis on disease prevention should be of the highest priority in a truly comprehensive study by the commission members.

Let the commission take time to research cost effective solutions, with input from all sections of American society.

During investigatory discussions with people from all walks of life concerning the American health care system and why it so expensive, the following four points have often come up, quite apart from the problems and issues discussed in the previous chapter.

1. The eating habits of Americans, and the cheap availability of fast food

2. The misconception that Sweden, France, and some other rich European countries are homogeneous societies, and do not have a foreign-born population.

3. The effect of legal and illegal immigration into the United States

4. The fact that America is such a large country, with over 300 million people

Each of the above points, especially number one, have some relevance in the context of health care costs, but points two, three, and four, have virtually no impact on them. I have not come across any authentic data from any reliable institution or authority that clearly states that these points are to any extent responsible for the high cost of health care in the United States. Following is a look at each of these points in some detail.

1.      It is a fact that the people of the United States eat more unhealthy 'fast food', that often their food habits are irregular, and that they tend to eat much larger portions than the average people of other rich countries do. Americans also tend to swallow their food on the run without taking the time to properly chew or digest it. They do this while standing, walking, or in eccentric cases, while running or driving. American eating habits are not healthy. However, in Japan people smoke too much, in France they drink too much wine, and in Germany they drink too much beer—each country has its excesses that drive up the cost of health care.

2.      The United States is a new nation built upon immigration in the last few centuries, and its population now exceeds 300 million people. Nearly 36 million of the American populace is foreign born. That is just 12%. Many of the other rich countries of Europe, as well as Australia and Canada, also have a foreign-born population of 10–15%. Therefore, the argument that somehow non-homogeneity leads to higher costs in health care does not hold validity. There is no authentic data that confirms, either way, whether the homogeneous nature of a population leads to lower costs in health care, or not. The argument of the 'homogeneity factor' and its relationship to health care costs remains unsubstantiated.

3.      As mentioned in the previous chapter, legal or illegal immigrants live longer than the native-born population of the United States. On average, these immigrants are younger and less likely to use health care facilities than native-born Americans are, although regionally, health care services are, to an extent, stretched in states bordering Mexico, where over 60% of illegal immigrants come from. The idea that immigrants raise the cost of health care for the entire nation is another myth.

4.      Another argument that is applied is that with America being such a large country, it is difficult to have a health care system that is not costly. The health care system could be

administered on a state-by-state basis though, rather than being centrally controlled. Japan has a population of nearly 140 million, which is much larger than the population of any of the individual states yet their health care system is efficient and nearly 100% cheaper per person than America's system is.

The above points are mentioned because people from all sections of society tend to have certain misconceptions as to why the current American health care system is so costly, per person, in relation to other rich countries. The effect of these misconceptions, particularly regarding points two, three, and four, which are greatly exaggerated in importance by certain decision makers and politicians, is that they make some of the population fearful of any change in the nation's health care system.

## Prevention and regular physical examination reduce the cost of health care (especially for people over forty years of age)

*Prevention of disease or illness is a necessary part of evolving a new and cost effective health care system. It is important that federal, state and city governments spend adequate money to educate people on the importance of a healthy diet, eating at regular times, essential daily exercise, and making an effort to reduce stress and conflict in their daily lives.*
The effects of smoking have been linked to cancer, heart disease, and other illnesses. Cigarette smoking used to be a common sight in almost every bar, restaurant, and public place, in all the rich countries. There have been significant steps towards reducing the use of tobacco, either by regulations, or by persistent advertising of the harmful effects of smoking, in the United States and other countries worldwide. Certainly, children should be made aware of the harmful effects of smoking at an early age, and this process must continue in order to cut down health care costs.
Only thirty to forty years ago, not many people wore seat belts in automobiles. These days almost all the people in western societies wear them while driving. There has been a marked

reduction of fatalities in car accidents because of this. Again, the wearing of seat belts was brought about by the constant education of people through various forms of advertising, and by creating rules and laws that made the wearing of seat belts mandatory in all the rich countries of the world.

The federal government issued guidelines in late 2008 to help people live healthier lifestyles, which in turn could help to slow soaring health care costs. These guidelines focus on proper levels of physical activity. Guidelines already existed for peoples' eating habits. Previously, Mike Leavitt, Secretary for Health and Human Resources, challenged the beverage and snack industry, as well as marketing and media groups, to reform their advertising campaigns in order to help create a 'culture of wellness'— essentially healthy living styles.

In most OECD countries, spending on health care accounted for more than 90% of total health spending, while promotional activities for healthy living styles represented less than 5% of that spending (OECD, 2003 d). The same OECD report stated that spending on the promotion of 'healthy living activities' was far below 5% of total spending for health care in the United States.

An urgent and massive effort by federal, state, and county governments, along with the private sector, is required in order to educate children in schools, students in colleges, and the population in general, on the benefit that daily exercise and healthy eating habits have on their health. The campaign for exercise and a healthy diet must be conducted more consistently and with more vigor than previous campaigns about the harmful effects of cigarette smoking and not wearing seat belts. Educating people about the benefits of exercise and a healthy diet will not only lead to a big reduction in health care costs, but also to improvement in the quality of their lives for many years to come.

President Clinton was a regular jogger during his years in office, but often he ate substantial amounts of fast food, including double portions of burgers and fries. A few years after his presidency, he had to have quadruple by-pass heart surgery. Doctors mostly blamed his heart disease on unhealthy food habits. He now follows a healthy diet (presumably watched closely by his doctors and his wife). In the last few years he has actively promoted the benefits of a healthy diet and food in American schools. County and state officials in many parts of the U.S. are beginning to remove chips, sodas, and other unhealthy snacks from the vending machines in schools. The campaign to educate people on the benefits of exercise and a healthy diet must spread to all elements of society.

Stress and personal conflicts in daily life contribute to illnesses. Grown up individuals should be made aware by doctors and other educators that it is essential to lessen, or even eliminate, stress and conflicts as far as it is possible to do so. Thinking positively helps in that respect. John Robbins[6], author of *Healthy at 100,* writes in his book "It has been said that we can destroy ourselves with negativity just as effectively as with bombs. People don't grow old: when they stop growing, they become old."

In the Scandinavian countries of Norway, Sweden, Finland, Denmark, and Iceland, people over forty are encouraged, sometimes by mandatory rules, to have regular physical check-ups. Most of the people in these countries comply. Failing to recommend something similar in the United States strongly is hard to understand. Regular physical check-ups can diagnose impending diseases and other medical problems in people, which would surely lead to lower health care costs. It is a preventive measure for enjoying a healthy life. If a disease or a health problem is discovered in its initial stages everybody knows about it, and something can often be done. Implementing a policy of physical check-ups past a certain age should be part and parcel of the health care system in America.

In the foreword of John Robbins' book, it states:

> With an emphasis on simple, wholesome, but satisfying fare, and the addition of a manageable daily exercise routine, many people can experience great improvement in the quality of

---

[6]  *Apart from his many accomplishments, John Robbins is the author of the million-copy bestseller Diet for a New America and Healthy at 100. His work has been the subject of cover stories and feature articles in The San Francisco Chronicle, The Los Angeles Times, The Washington Post, The New York Times, and People.*

their lives, now and for many years to come. But most surprising is Robbins' discovery that it is not diet and exercise alone that help people to live well past one hundred. The quality of personal relationships is enormously important. Robbins asserts that loneliness has more impact on life-span than such known vices as smoking. There is clearly a strong beneficial power to love and connection.

*Prevention*—real prevention—has an important role in making a health care system for all affordable, as well as in substantially reducing administrative and medical costs.

The United States of America currently wins the contest for being the fattest nation among the twenty-four OECD developed nations. The U.S. ranks number one in obesity for both men and women according to the OECD report "Health at a Glance" issued in Paris in 2001. For people over fifteen years old, the figure shows that 25.1% of American females and 19.9% of American males had a BMI (Body Mass Index) over 30. Both are much higher than the numbers for the other twenty-three OECD countries. A BMI of over thirty is in the 'obese' category, and leads to many chronic diseases and illnesses. There are many factors in American life, such as physical inactivity and junk food eating habits, which have contributed to this trend in the American population. It is time to take accelerated steps in order to reduce obesity. It will not only lead to increased productivity in the nation but will also reduce the cost of health care.

Following is a summation of the essential criteria for preventive points:

- It is important that federal, state, and city governments, and the private sector, substantially increase their budgets to educate people on the importance of eating a healthy diet at regular times and getting essential daily exercise, and to encourage people to reduce stress and conflict in their daily lives.

- It is essential to advocate and even preach positive thinking for the reduction of stress and conflict amongst the population.

- Make regular exercise in schools part of the curriculum while students are in college, and encourage the public to exercise regularly, instead of watching sports on television. When people watch spectator sports, invariably they eat junk food and often drink alcoholic or syrupy beverages.

- Junk food has become part of the American psyche. Replace junk food, unhealthy snacks, and sodas with healthy food and drinks in the vending machines at schools and universities.

- Encourage regular health checks at every level, especially for people over forty years of age.

- Discourage smoking and excessive drinking.

Whichever universal health care system America adopts—whether it is a mixture of public and private financing or it is publicly financed predominantly—healthy lifestyles, healthy diet, exercise, and prevention are the key ingredients of any health care system. Both public and private sectors must embark on a massive education campaign.

## OECD guidelines for action

The 2005 OECD Health Project report, "Towards High-Performing Health Systems" makes certain recommendations in direction for health policy. The authors report that:

> The pay-off from years of experimentation and investigation is that health policy makers in OECD countries now know quite a bit about which tools and approaches can be used successfully to accomplish many key policy objectives, such as controlling the rate of public spending growth, ensuring equitable access to care, im-

proving health and preventing disease, and establishing equitable and sustainable financing
for health and long-term care services.

The OECD's summary of their directions for health policy
follow. It should be noted, "One size does not fit all" in the health
care systems of the rich countries of the world, and that policies
should be adjusted according to the operating health care system of
a particular country.

*Possible lines of action for improving health status and
health outcomes of the population*

- Employ well-designed strategies to prevent illness and
  disability, which may entail reallocation of health-system
  resources from care to prevention, or changes in the way
  resources are spent.

- Address inequities in health care through initiatives targeted at
  attacking root causes, such as poverty and social exclusion.

- Support efforts to increase the extent to which medical practice
  is consistent with evidence—including the development
  and implementation of evidence-based guidelines and
  performance standards.

- Ensure that systems for monitoring the quality of health and
  long-term care are sufficient to assist in meeting improvement
  goals.

*Possible lines of action for fostering adequate and equitable
access to care*

- Eliminate financial barriers to access by providing or
  subsidizing health care coverage for the poor, exempting
  poor persons from patient cost-sharing requirements, and
  allowing complementary private insurance to cover a portion
  of the user's fees in cases that create access barriers.

- Foster access to affordable private health insurance by high-risk persons who need such coverage, (e.g., the elderly and those with costly medical conditions) through policy interventions such as targeted regulations, subsidies, or fiscal incentives.

- Avoid unintended inequities in access by persons with different sources of health coverage, through policy interventions such as universally applicable provider reimbursement limits or employment of common waiting lists.

*Possible lines of action for increasing health-system responsiveness*

- Improve recipient satisfaction with long-term care, by supporting family caregivers to increase care recipients' control over services and choice of providers, and/or by offering cash payments for spending on services directly to those eligible for benefits.

- Facilitate informed consumer choice of health insurance coverage, whether publicly or privately financed.

*Possible lines of action for ensuring sustainable costs and financing*

- Moderate the rate of growth in public spending on health through a combination of budgetary and administrative controls over payments, prices, or supply of services. Monitor carefully the effects of such interventions on health-system performance.

- Add modest cost-sharing requirements to publicly financed health coverage schemes, and bar complementary health insurance from covering, in full, the amount to be paid by the patient.

- Eliminate public coverage for ancillary or luxury services, allowing for rationing by price and optional risk pooling, through privately financed supplementary coverage.

- Possible lines of action for increasing the efficiency of health systems

- Manage demand for elective surgery and other discretionary care, through gatekeepers (doctors' offices), clinical prioritization, or consumer and patient information schemes, particularly in systems where low patient cost-sharing and excess supply of health-care providers combine to promote high levels of service use.

- Employ pharmaceutical pricing systems and other policies that reward cost-effective choices among similar medications, and encourage truly novel innovation in the pharmaceutical sector.

- Use technology assessment to promote informed decision-making, use technology-management approaches that consider health outcomes, and promote cost-effective health-care delivery.

- Develop, test, and employ payment systems for health-care services that reward productivity and quality.

- Invest in automated health-data systems needed to improve the organization and delivery of health care. The burden of cost for the equipment should not be on the doctor's practice.

Many of the above policy directions could be used in a universal health care system adapted to the individual states of America. Bear in mind that competitive market forces and medical technologies can be employed to increase the efficiency of health care systems. Economic incentives to health care providers can also be used, as long as they are aligned with the goals of cost-effective health care delivery.

**Evolving concepts of universal health care in the United States**

People often say to me that the United States is too large of a country in which to administer a universal health care system with coverage for every resident, because the system will be too bureaucratic, and because socialized medicine is not the solution to the nation's health care problems.

I agree that if the health care system is federally controlled and managed it will become too bureaucratic, and will not cater to the health care needs of the residents of each state. However, socialized medicine is a cliché term used by certain politicians and interest groups in this most capitalistic economy, in order to strike negative thought in people's minds. Why don't people realize that the United States military is an example of a socialized system? Funded through direct taxation, it has a central command system, and is responsible for the combined security of the nation. These same principles apply to a universal system that gives health care security to all, without a change of ideology. It is how the Scandinavian countries have created their health care systems, which are superior, and cover each resident at a much lower cost per person than in America.

One problem is that many people do not understand the distinction between the terms 'universal' and 'single-payer.' Single-payer merely means that health care services are paid for from a single source that is established and managed by the government, while in a universal system the funding *can* come from a single-payer, or it can come from a combination of both public and private funds. The other problem is that the term single-payer has been branded with a socialized connotation, whereas in truth it refers only to the fact that coverage is funded by a single source, such as taxation, as in Medicare. In order to fit the definition of 'socialized,' health services would also have to be provided by government employees, as in the VHA. Therefore, the difference is not in how it is funded, but in who provides the services.

The American health care system is money driven. In its current form, it can neither provide health care to each person, nor can it control rising costs. In its current structure, it is unsustainable and needs a complete overhaul.

The federal government and Congress should set overall policy goals for a universal health care system. Let each state government then decide, with the consent of its residents, which type of system is the best to be implemented in their state. There are three choices:

- A single-payer system wherein the residents would receive universal health care, such as the California Health Insurance Reliability Act, SB 840.

- A universal health care system funded by public and private means, such as the Massachusetts Health Care Reform Plan.

- A universal health care system that is either a version of the proposed California system or a version of the Massachusetts Plan, with top-up insurance plans, and that covers each resident of the state.

In order to further develop the cost effective terms of health care of the above three systems, the commission and the federal government should take into consideration the health care systems of Norway, Sweden, France, Australia, Japan, and a few other rich countries, and how the best quality health care is being dispensed fairly, to the consumers in those societies. The named countries in this paragraph have some of the finest health care systems in the world according to The World Health Organization (WHO) and OECD.

All the funds currently allocated to fragmented federal entitlement programs should be appropriated to each state of the union according to certain criteria of the population, cost, and other parameters, which are agreed upon between the federal and state governments. Each state should then be allowed to manage and run their universal health care system by one of the three above-mentioned choices.

The residents of each state should be able to receive health care in the other states of the union—as is being done in many European Union (EU) countries. For example, the residents of Germany can get treatment in France, Belgium, and Sweden, amongst others countries. Most residents of EU countries carry an electronic health care card for this purpose. The federal government and states of the union could also have reciprocal health care arrangements for their residents with EU countries. In this way, citizens of the U.S traveling to the EU could receive treatment if they were taken ill or met with an unfortunate accident while traveling there. Similarly, the procedures could be reciprocal for EU residents visiting the United States.

# Additional recommendations

**American infant mortality is a disgrace for a rich country—but the solution is there**

Singapore has the best infant survival rate in the world—2.3 babies die before the age of one for every thousand live births. Iceland, Japan and Sweden all have a rate that is less than half that of America. Nicholas D. Kristof wrote in the *New York Times* of January 13, 2005, that "Here's a wrenching fact: If the United States had an infant mortality rate *as good as Cuba's,* we would save an additional 2,212 American babies a year." He went on to add, "Yes, Cuba's. Babies are less likely to survive in America, with a health care system that we think is the best in the world, than in impoverished and autocratic Cuba."

The American infant mortality rate is around seven babies for every thousand live births, dying before the age of one. According to the CIA *World Factbook of 2008*, Cuba is one of forty-one countries that have a better infant mortality rate than the United States has. Even China has managed to drive down the rate in Beijing to 4.6 per thousand. In contrast, New York City's rate is 6.5. What is even more amazing is that women are 70% more likely to die in childbirth in America than in Europe, according to Kristof's article.

What is most disturbing is that those politicians and decision makers who preach so much about 'pro-life'— are the same people who have done little to look at a universal health care system in America that could reduce the infant mortality rate. It is a paradox—'pro-life' talk goes on while living babies could be saved from death.

Why don't the state and federal governments send a delegation of experts to countries like Singapore and Sweden, to learn the reasons for their low infant mortality rates, and then implement those best practices in the America health care system? If nearly 19,000 babies a year would be saved if America brought down its infant mortality rate to that of Singapore, then surely this would be a good investment of our experts' time.

## Role of information technology (IT) and outsourcing

In the United States, paperwork, inefficient communications, and bureaucracy riddle the health care system. In some estimates, it costs as much as 20–30% of the total health care expenditure of over 2 trillion dollars, while these costs are less than 10% of the total expenditure in the health care systems of other rich countries in the world. Extensive use of information technology can cut down the cost of health care. Dr. David J. Brailer, National Coordinator of Health Care IT, U.S. Department of Health and Human Services, organized a group of CEOs in 2005 that included FedEx's Frederick Smith and PepsiCo's Steven Reinmund to talk about the effect of extensive use of IT in the health care industry. They came up with the conclusion that nearly 30% of U.S health care spending could be cut by using IT effectively.

There is a need to incorporate a confidential electronic network of health information for each patient in the health care system, thus eliminating unnecessary paperwork and cutting down on medical errors. In an efficient IT health care system, patient records would simultaneously be available to all appropriate health care providers—and *only* to health care providers.

All office work—including billing, diagnosing, prescribing, and other areas—can be much more efficiently organized by effectively using IT technologies.

## Web-based, cost effective, medical solutions

There are several ways that web-based communications can effectively reduce the cost of health care. Some of these suggestions are listed below:

- Doctor-patient relationship: Doctors and patients could communicate directly, by either email or video conferencing (at some point in the future), whereby the patient could let the doctor know his or her symptoms, and then the doctor could prescribe a suitable remedy. This would certainly work in cases where the doctor and patient already have a good confidential relationship, and have built up mutual trust. Of course, the doctor could not do it if the patient's symptoms required more than verbal or visual screening. In the next few years, it may become easier for patients to visually see and talk with doctors directly, via their computers. An equivalent version of that would be the videoconferences of today. Doctors could devote a few hours of fixed time per week to communicating with their patients on-line.

- Doctors could email patients their repeat prescriptions. This would save time on the part of doctor as well as of the patient. Again, it would require a kind of trust between the doctor and the patient.

- Health clinics on the web: Health clinics on the web would consist of specialized, accredited doctors who could give a diagnosis and then suggest treatment for a patient's inquiry, directly online or by email. Web-based clinics could charge small fees for such a service, which understandably, would only be for non-emergency cases. A few web-based sites provide limited services in this way already. Two examples are www.hellomd.com and www.webmd.com.

Another interesting website is from the National Health Service in England. It gives an introduction, symptoms, causes, diagnosis, treatment, complications, and references to thousands of human conditions and diseases. Anyone can check their symptoms or find a useful remedy for their condition, by clicking "Health A-Z" before visiting a doctor. This can save time for both doctors and patients. The health services of some other affluent nations also have similar sites.

**Medical tourism can assist in cost cutting**

'Medical Tourist' is a term that has arisen from the rapid growth of an industry where people from all over the world are traveling to other countries to obtain medical, dental, and surgical care, while touring, vacationing, and fully experiencing, the attractions of the countries they are visiting at the same time. Medical tourism can also be broadly defined as the provision of cost-effective private medical care, in collaboration with the tourist industry, for patients needing surgical and other forms of specialized treatment that they cannot afford where they live.

The so-called medical tourist industry is only a few years old. Most tourists arrange their plans through special agencies or with the foreign hospitals themselves. There is plenty of information available about particular hospitals and agencies dealing with medical patients on the Internet.

Extensive use of medical technology is essential in testing, treatment, procedures, and operations on a patient. The cost of this technology is becoming increasingly prohibitive in the United States. Millions of people from rich countries in the world are seeking medical care in India, Mexico, Thailand, Malaysia, Singapore, Brazil, Costa Rica, Poland, Turkey, and some other economically developing nations.

People from America and other rich countries can get elective procedures such as cosmetic surgery, hip and knee replacements, dental procedures, infertility treatments, and any other procedure not usually covered by insurance or that has a long waiting time in their home countries.

National Public Radio (NPR) reported on November 14, 2007, that Americans faced with rising health care costs are digging out their passports for treatment abroad. It is estimated that between 500,000 and 1 million Americans go abroad to get advanced medical care from lower-priced hospitals and clinics in countries like India, Thailand and Mexico.

*The Journal of Financial Planning* estimates that savings may range from 50–95% of the U.S. cost for procedures and surgery done abroad, and this includes the cost of travel, accommodation, and other expenses.

Author Josef Woodman writes in *Patients Beyond Borders*:

> If you're seeking cosmetic surgery, Brazil, Costa Rica and South Africa rank among the most popular destinations, while dentistry will have you exploring Mexico, Costa Rica, or Hungary. The more expensive, invasive surgeries, such as open-heart surgery or a knee replacement, make a longer trip to India, Thailand, Singapore, or Malaysia well worth the cost, time and distance of travel.

CBS *60 Minutes* correspondent Bob Simon had a program on September 4, 2005, called "Vacation, Adventure, and Surgery?" This program revealed some of the experiences of American patients who went to India for surgery. Following are of the experiences of two patients from the U.K and the U.S.

Anne Bell worked at the British High Commission in New Delhi. She had a baby at a private hospital there. She was glad that the delivery happened in India, and not in England. Ann had no pressure to go home after the birth of the baby, and she was welcomed to stay as long as she wished. The hospital staff looked after the baby and Ann, giving her enough time to settle and gain confidence. In England, and in America, the patient would be out of the hospital within a day if it were a normal delivery. It is unlikely also, to have a private room with a private bath in England, but massages and yoga were thrown in as well while she was recovering, quite apart from the fact that the whole thing cost a lot less than it would have in England.

Another patient, Stephanie Sedlmayr, flew from Vero Beach, FL, to the Apollo Hospital in Bombay for a hip operation, which was too expensive in the U.S. as she was uninsured. Stephanie told *60 Minutes* that she did not just go there to save money; she came for an operation she could not get at home. This particular hip procedure is called 'hip surfacing.' The FDA has not approved this kind of operation, but in India, Dr. Vijay Bose has performed over

300 of them. He showed *60 Minutes* the difference between a hip resurfacing and hip replacement, which is the standard operation performed in the United States. Dr. Bose stated that his patients usually recover faster because his procedure is far less radical and does not involve cutting the thighbone. Instead, Bose fits a metal cap over the end, which fits into a metal socket in the hip. The result, he says, is that patients end up with enough mobility to do virtually anything. It is estimated that such a hip replacement procedure would cost nearly $35,000 in the U.S., while it only costs $5,800 in India, which included a private nurse and the hospital room. By the time 60 minutes left India, Stephanie was into the tourism part of her treatment, convalescing at a seaside resort an hour's drive from the hospital.

*YaleGlobal Online* reported in 2008:

> Take the rising popularity of 'preventive health screening.' At one private clinic in London, a thorough men's health check-up that includes blood tests, electro-cardiogram tests, chest x-rays, lung tests, and abdominal ultrasound, costs nearly £345 ($574, €500). By comparison, a comparable check-up at a clinic operated by Delhi-based healthcare company Max Healthcare costs $84.

It would probably cost more than $1,000 in the United States.

With the liberalization of the Indian economy, private health care took off in a big way. Entrepreneurs willing to take an uncompromising view on the quality of health care for their patients fund it. Major health groups like Apollo Hospitals, Wockhardt, and Fortis are experiencing extraordinary expansion. New groups are also joining the rise of private health care in India. McKinsey, the global consulting firm, believes India's private health care industry will grow to $60 billion by 2012. This private health sector is already catering to medical tourists.

Dr. Prathap C Reddy, founder and Chairman of Apollo Hospitals Group, states that the mission of Apollo Group is, "to bring healthcare of international standards within the reach of every individual. We are committed to the achievement and maintenance of excellence in education, research, and healthcare, for the benefit of humanity."

The Apollo Group is the largest health care group in Asia, the third largest in the world, and the most important player attracting American medical tourists. It has over 8,000 beds in more than 40 hospitals, a string of nursing and hospital management colleges, and dual pharmacy and diagnostic clinic lifelines, providing a safety net across Asia. The American non-profit organization, Joint Commission International (JCI), accredits some hospitals in the Apollo Group. JCI accredits hospitals in the United States, and has an international division that does the same thing for foreign hospitals and other health care facilities. The number of international entities accredited by JCI has grown to over 300, and most of these are in Asia.

India offers opportunities for both medical tourists and insurance companies to cut the cost of health care in America. It also has several added advantages as presented below:

- India's corporate sector is involved in medical care as well as the tourist industry, both private and public. It provides low cost, budget friendly medical procedures.

- India has some of the most highly qualified, experienced, and internationally acknowledged doctors in the world. Most of the physicians have had additional hands-on training at leading medical centers throughout the U.S, Europe, and other countries.

- There is zero waiting time for various procedures and surgeries.

- Most of the doctors speak English.

- In addition to traditional medicine, India offers many relaxing and rejuvenating treatment options, from yoga, ayurvedic medicine, and meditation, to allopathic and naturopathic medicine.

Apollo hospitals became a pioneer in helping people to maintain physical, mental, and emotional well-being by launching the first Wellness Center at Apollo Hospital, Chennai, in February 2005. The Wellness Plus program offered by the center is defined by Apollo as:

- A perfect blend of modern and complementary medicine— the latest medical techniques combined with ancient healing methods like aromatherapy, pranic healing, yoga, and meditation.

- Completely authentic and scientific

- Offering complete solutions for lifestyle modification ranging from prevention of disease, control of disease symptoms, and anti-aging solutions

Details of every medical procedure and service, with costs, are listed at the Apollo website, which caters to 15 million patients from all over the world.

Some of the major U.S. insurance companies such as Aetna, Cigna, and Humana, are considering incorporating JCI accredited hospitals into their health insurance policies for Americans, in order to cut ever-increasing costs. A few smaller insurance companies offer incentives for their patients to have medical treatment abroad. For uninsured and under-insured middle class Americans, it may become the only way to get medical treatment if their condition does not entail immediate urgency. Some insurance companies already offer clients living in border states both dental and surgical treatment in Mexico—as it can be 16–25% of the cost of having the same treatment or procedure in the United States.

Some health plans in Southern California already offer lower premiums and co-payments to patients who use network providers in Mexico. For several years, Blue Shield of California has offered an HMO plan, Access Baja, in which enrollees visit physicians across the border in Tijuana. The premiums for Access Baja are less than two-thirds the cost of the alternative Blue Shield of California plans, as medical costs are much lower in Mexico.

Many economically developing countries like Thailand, Mexico, and India offer these treatments at costs that are sometimes less than one-tenth of those in the United States. The following table presents the approximate cost of each treatment in private hospitals and clinics in India.

Figure 16

| Treatment | Cost |
|---|---|
| Pediatric heart surgery    Single valve:<br>Double valve: | $ 6,600<br>$ 7,480 |
| Angioplasty | $ 4,400 |
| Total knee replacement | $ 3,380 |
| Total hip replacement | $ 3,605 |
| Diabetic check | $ 100 |
| Whole body check | $ 200 |
| Heart check | $ 155 |
| Breast reconstruction | $ 3,740 |
| Face lift | $ 2,860 |
| Scar revision | $ 450 |
| Cheek implant | $ 1,010 |
| Angiography procedure | $ 615 |
| In most cases, the package cost includes operating charges, accommodation, inpatient nursing charges, service charges, doctors' fees, meals/laundry, airport pick-up and drop-off, one-day local sightseeing for attendant by AC car, interpreter when required, embassy contact when required, and local transport. | |

Source: India Abroad June 24, 2005

Njay Krishnan wrote an article titled, "Want That Cardiac Surgery Done? Go to India!" in *India Abroad* on June 24, 2005. He gives many examples of Americans getting treatment in hospitals in India.

He wrote, "For instance, in April the Madras Medical Mission Hospital in Chennai, set up by renowned cardiologist Dr K M Cherian, performed a complicated cardiac procedure on an eighty-seven year old American. The total cost worked out to about $8,000, inclusive of airfares and a thirty-day stay in the hospital." The cost of such a procedure would probably be ten to fifteen times that in the United States.

It is expected that new medical tourism will generate billions of dollars for India, according to the *Financial Times*. Several prominent consulting groups like McKinsey and other known institutions estimate that the medical tourism industry will generate anything between a few billion dollars to 30 billion dollars annually for India by the year 2012.

Today medical tourism is only a trickle, but it is likely to turn into a flood if the cost of health care keeps rising by double-digit numbers in the United States. With the effective use of IT, America could cut down on the cost of health care by sending patients not in need of emergency treatment to countries like Mexico and India, thereby saving an enormous amount of money.

Andres Oppenheimer wrote in the *Miami Herald* on August 14, 2007:

> So far, while China, India and several other developing countries have JCI-accredited hospitals, in the Americas outside the United States and Canada only hospitals in Brazil and Bermuda have reached that level, according to the JCI Web page. (Mexico, Costa Rica and Panama, among others, are applying for accreditation.)

Thailand has become another important country attracting medical tourists. People all over the world have been traveling to Thailand, known for its Buddhas, its beaches, its brothels, its foods, and the bustle of Bangkok, for exotic vacations. Chris Taylor wrote in the *Financial Times* of June 6, 2007, "Medical Tourism is becoming more popular as health costs rise and baby boomers age into increasing problems." Arnold Milstein, chief physician for the consulting firm Mercer Health and Benefits predicts, "The best offshore hospitals will routinely be included in networks offered to insured hospitals."

While India and Thailand attract the lion's share of Medical Tourism, Josef Woodman, author of *Patients Beyond Borders*, suggests Singapore could actually be the best value for money. The World Health Organization ranks it sixth in the world for healthcare, and several of its hospitals are JCI-accredited.

Many medical tourist patients have expressed sentiments similar to, "they pick you up, take you to the airport, fly you in, and accompany you to all the operations. Then you are at a five star hotel to recuperate."

The Bumrungrad Hospital, Bangkok, is a luxurious place that claims to have more foreign patients than any other hospital in the world. It is JCI-accredited. The hospital is like a United Nations of patients. They are cared for by more than 500 doctors, most of them with international training. Curt Schroeder, CEO of Bumrungrad, said that the hospital took in more than 350,000 international patients in the year 2004–05. Most of the doctors at the hospital graduated from U.S. medical schools.

Correspondent Bob Simon of *60 Minutes* described the experiences of two of the American patients that were treated at Bumrungrad Hospital. Byron Bonnewell, who had heart bypass surgery, and Kim Atwater, who had an eyelift, both were full of praise for their treatment. Not only had it cost them an eighth of what the surgery would have cost in the United States, but they also described their positive experience at the hospital as beyond their expectations. Atwater stated that her stay at Bumrungrad Hospital was much nicer than any she had experienced in the United States, and that the rooms looked more like hotel rooms than hospital rooms, and came with excellent service.

There are tips that the American medical tourist should seriously consider before departing for treatment abroad. They can be summed up as follows:

- Make sure of the cost of your surgery or procedure, whether it includes your stay in the hospital, all other services provided by the hospital, as well as including time for recuperation.

- Check whether the hospital is JCI-accredited.

- Inform your insurance company about the treatment abroad. If the company is willing to foot the bill, have this confirmed in writing.

- Find out who your surgeon at the foreign hospital will be, and speak with the surgeon one to one on the telephone before your departure.

- Take your medical records. If any issues arise then your doctor in the U.S. will be fully aware of the situation. Make sure what has to be done, and what aftercare will be required.

- Arrive a few days early to acclimatize yourself to local time and weather conditions.

- You should be aware that litigation for malpractice is not the same as in the U.S. It works within the laws of that particular country.

More and more uninsured and under-insured Americans are traveling to Mexico for treatments that are comparable to care found in the United States, and at far lower prices. Americans are going to Mexico for reasons such as being denied treatment by their insurers and because of the prohibitively high cost of dentistry, private doctors, and hospitals. Dental treatment in Mexico is the one most favored by Americans.

According to a study conducted by the University of Texas Medical Center in El Paso, more than 20 million U.S./Mexico border crossings made annually are for medical care. Milica Bookman, professor of economics at St. Joseph University in Philadelphia, and co-author of the book *Medical Tourism in Developing Countries*, thinks part of the attraction is Mexico's closeness to the United States. "Central and South American countries have a huge advantage over Asian destinations as a result of their proximity," Bookman explained. "Traveling there for health care entails a shorter time." This is especially true for the border states of California, Texas, New Mexico, and Arizona.

In this age of globalization, we have already seen manufacturing and information technology jobs moving from the United States to developing economies like India, China, and Mexico, amongst others. IBM alone employs nearly 80,000 people in India, which is nearly 20% of its workforce worldwide. Most consumer goods manufactured in China now, and then imported into America. As companies globalize, they will move their plants and IT jobs to places where labor is cheaper. The same will happen on a large scale with medical tourists, as they to go to countries where they can get substantially cheaper treatment for non-emergency surgeries or procedures. This will inevitably cut down the cost of health care in the United States. We are already witnessing insurance companies that are offering policies with lower premiums and co-payments for their clients in the states bordering Mexico.

It does not matter what form of universal health care eventually evolves in the different states across America. Whether it be a single-payer system, or one funded by a combination of public and private funds, state and federal governments and insurance companies will need to send their medical clients abroad for non-emergency treatment in order to combat rising costs.

**Biotech in emerging countries can help to cut costs**

The ever-increasing price of drugs, another issue that confronts people in America, also plays a part in health care costs. Indian biotech companies cannot only enhance global health, but can be key players in reducing the cost of drugs.

Suman Guha Mozumder wrote in *India Abroad* on April 20, 2007:

> India has a huge potential to improve the health of humankind, thanks to its biotech firms emerging as global players with the know-how to produce innovative generic drugs and vaccines

215

at lower costs than Western multinationals. This is the conclusion of groundbreaking research by McLaughlin-Rotman Center for Global Health (Health Network of University of Toronto), announced last week by the prestigious Nature Biotechnology.

The research by McLaughlin-Rotman Center further states that the global market for generic biopharmaceuticals will increase significantly in the coming years as several blockbuster drugs lose patent protection. Indian companies are well positioned to reduce costs of these drugs by cornering some of the market share, and then competing on a global scale. The same study states, "The launch of the hepatitis B vaccine developed by Shantha Biotechnics led to a thirty-fold domestic price reduction—from about $15 for a comparable product to roughly $0.50 in India."

The biotech industry in India is following in the footsteps of the IT industry.

Peter A. Singer, co-author of the research, stated to *India Abroad*, "India is innovating its way out of poverty and with a massive and increasingly well-educated workforce, the country is poised to revolutionize biotechnology. The Indian biotech sector is like a baby elephant – when it matures, it will occupy a lot of space."

There is no doubt that the cost of drugs will start to decline within a decade as biotech industries develop in emerging markets like India. This will be good news for reducing the cost of health care in America in the coming years. Western drug companies are already moving to make alliances with local companies in emerging markets, in the same way western IT companies did before.

**Alternative Medicine**

A highly motivated nation, eager to reduce health care costs even more dramatically, could take lessons from what we have learned about good health and longevity on the planet over thousands of years. The principles of prevention and longevity were proven long before Congress passed Medicare and implemented it in 1967.

The most expensive drugs fail to work well because of a sad lack of critical knowledge. It may be that drug designers want proprietary drugs that work for a limited time, need repeated doses, with side effects requiring other pills to control them.

It is time for the United States to incorporate certain other forms of alternative medicine and therapies like allopathic, homeopathic, and herbal medicine, as well as acupuncture, into the health care system. Proven alternative medicine can be useful for patients, have fewer side effects, and can only be cost effective.

## Issues necessary to cut the cost of health care and make it efficient

Some of the most important issues mentioned would require either regulation or legislation by federal and state governments.

### Fragmented federal and state entitlement programs

There are major problems with entitlement programs funded and run by either the federal government, state governments, or by a combination of both—all lead to a great deal of paperwork and the net effect is the inefficient delivery of health care. These problems have already been discussed in chapter 5. All these programs should be eliminated and be replaced by a single program that takes into consideration the needs of the military, as well as the elderly, poor, and other vulnerable groups that are unable to contribute in taxation or otherwise to the general funding of the health care system.

The health care systems of England and other European countries have special provisions for the treatment of vulnerable groups, i.e., elderly, poor, unemployed, handicapped, children, students, and working military personnel, and for how they pay for prescription drugs. Further development of the three suggested universal health care systems for America on the preceding pages could include provisions similar to those of the EU health care systems in this respect.

There is no need to have special hospitals for veterans. The integration of the existing 175 or more VA hospitals under one universal health care system would lessen bureaucracy and paperwork. Military personnel and their dependants could then go to any hospital of their choice, instead of being restricted to VA hospitals. Over-burdened hospitals would be able to transfer their patients to hospitals that had excess capacity. Currently, such interchangeability is not possible.

**Politicians and lobbyists**

Cost effective reform of health care would be much easier if health care industry lobbyists were banned from contributing money to legislators and their staff in order to maintain their power. These lobbyists have undue influence over politicians, against the wishes of the people—it is neither healthy for a mature democracy, nor it is conducive to developing a cost effective health care system. The current system is money driven. Lobbyists corrupt politicians and their staff for the benefit of their part of the health industry—this is common sense, well known to every citizen. Few such lobbyists exist in the rich countries of Europe. It is typically an American phenomenon.

**Health insurance industry and insurance policies**

There is no chance for health insurers to regulate themselves as long as the current health care system in America exists. Many doctors and patients complain that insurance company officials decide what kind of treatment, operation, or procedure, is suitable for a particular patient, instead of the decision being made in the best interest of the patient by a doctor. Often doctors and patients are left on hold on their phones for long periods of time while the low-level official of an insurance company tries to establish what kind of treatment or procedure is included in a particular patient's insurance policy. This can lead to an enormous amount of wasted time and paperwork, and to frustration for both medical staff and patients. Lavish remunerations to insurance executives, whose companies receive a fair amount of taxpayer money from state and federal governments, require tougher controls and regulations from authorities. The decisions about a patient's care must be left in the hands of doctors and not with insurance company bureaucrats.

In a single-payer universal health care system, there is no need for the health insurance industry, thereby saving enormous costs to the system by eliminating the 'middleman', or a layer of bureaucracy. In either a universal health care system with top-up insurance, or a system that accommodates both public and private financing like the Massachusetts Health Care Plan, the role of the health insurance industry should be more heavily regulated.

To cut down the cost of a universal health care system, insurance companies should be strictly regulated and be required to provide policies that are written in simple English without ambiguities. They should only be allowed to provide a limited number of policies and deductibles, and they should not be allowed to choose whom they would cover. Only a few companies should be able to provide health insurance in each state. This could be done by a bidding process—meaning they would bid for the cost of health insurance against each other and only the top three in each state would be selected to provide health insurance. By following this process, competition could be preserved while satisfying the needs of patients. The same process could have been applied to the entitlement program for prescription drugs, Medicare Part D, for seniors and the disabled.

## Cost of prescription drugs and their hyped advertisement

No residents or citizens of any other rich country pay as high a cost for prescription drugs as the residents of the United States. The cost of prescription drugs can be as much as 30 to 70 percent higher for American residents, compared to that of the residents of the other rich countries of Europe, Australia, Japan, and Canada. Why is this so? It is because in these countries, the state severely restricts the power of the drug companies to set their own prices. Government authorities dictate the bulk buying price of drugs (prescription or otherwise) that are sold in the pharmacies, and drug companies do not have the money or lobbying power to influence lawmakers and others involved in decision making processes related to the health care system.

The Veterans Administration (VA) directly negotiates the price of drugs with pharmaceutical companies in America, yet the Prescription Drug Plan D for seniors did not have this provision in the bill, which means that the VA is able to purchase prescription drugs at much lower prices for their patients than Plan D can for seniors. In other words, the legislators and the federal authorities gave away money to the drug and insurance companies.

The cost of drugs in America is out of control. It is based on the greed of the drug companies, not on traditional profit margins. The following example comes from personal experience.

I had a medical check up in October 2006 at a VA hospital. I stayed the night in my own very comfortable room with T.V. In the morning, I got into a discussion with the doctor about health care as I gave him my card about the book I was writing. I asked him why drug companies aggressively promote drugs such as those that lower cholesterol levels and blood pressure, and why these drugs are so expensive. I asked further, if there were effective alternatives to these drugs, and what kind of drugs patients took before Lipitor (for lowering cholesterol) came along. He mentioned the names of two drugs—one for blood pressure and the other for cholesterol—the latter costing less than one-tenth the price of Lipitor, which is $100 or more for a month's supply.

What are drug companies trying to achieve? Is it to create demand for their patented drugs when there is not even a disease, or when aspirin would work fine instead of an expensive state-of-the-art pain pill? The point I am trying to make is that there could be real cost cutting in health care if pharmaceutical companies did not create unnecessary demand for their hyped up drugs, which the patient may not even require.

In the same hospital, I received five to six forms, which I signed, and nearly fifty pages of information that I did not read! I thought this was not only a waste of paper, but also an added cost involved in processing a patient. Surely, the cost of paperwork and processing can be seriously reduced.

## Cost of malpractice lawsuits and insurance

America, where over 60% of the lawyers in the world reside, is the most litigious society in the world. Frivolous lawsuits brought against medical staff and hospitals are common in the American health care system. This results in not only driving up the cost of malpractice insurance, but leads doctors and medical staff to practice defensive medicine for fear of being sued. The net effect is that it increases the cost of health care. Defensive medicine means ordering excessive tests, avoiding risky procedures, and referring patients to see specialists when no such visit is really warranted by the medical evidence. There is nothing wrong with defensive medicine, but when this becomes routine for confirming even the simplest diagnosis of a patient, then the cost of health care rises, and it becomes a severe drain of resources in the health care system. Thus, it is urgent and important for legislators to take effective measures in order to eliminate frivolous lawsuits.

In the previous chapter, I made suggestions in this respect, and I repeat them here once more. Even the present health care system in America can be more cost effective by implementing, somehow, the following points.

- Law partners or lawyers should pay for the cost of bringing frivolous lawsuits if their cases are dismissed. There should be a cap on damages awarded in any particular case. Non-economic compensation should be according to a fixed schedule, instead of judges or jurors picking a figure from the air. Cases should be heard by specialized courts where judges are experts in complex health care problems and patients' conditions—thus excluding juries from hearing complex health care cases. Patients must be guaranteed at least 50% of the awards in any particular case.

- Ethical review committees, comprised of people of integrity, including doctors and lawyers, should deal with malpractice cases at local and state levels first, before cases against doctors, health care employees, and hospitals, are allowed to proceed in court.

It would certainly cut down the cost of health care if the above suggestions were given due consideration.

# CHAPTER VIII

## Conclusions

The United States is unique amongst the rich nations in that it has a fragmented, inefficient, and bureaucratically wasteful health care system that leaves over 47 million people uninsured and millions more under-insured. The major problems and issues afflicting the American health care system have been pointed out earlier in chapter 5.

The so-called socialized medicine myth promoted by some politicians, the media, and entrenched groups for their own self-interests has prevented America from developing an efficient single-payer universal health care system. However, key politicians, including President Obama, Senator Kennedy, Secretary of State Clinton, and Senator Tom Daschle, believe in their hearts it is the only system that will work for everyone. In an interview with Dr. Sanjay Gupta of CNN in March 2009, former President Bill Clinton said that $200 billion in health care spending could be saved annually, in a single-payer system, by cutting the costs of insurance companies as well as reducing the diffused responsibilities of medical service providers.

The obstacle to the acceptance of such as system is that America is the world's ultimate capitalistic society. Most Americans have been conditioned to believe that anything run by the government is socialistic, but they never refer to the American military machine as a 'socialistic army.' Why? After all, it is 100% funded by taxpayer money. So are the VA, Medicaid, and Medicare for that matter! Without this ideological interference, the same concept could be used to create a universal health care system. The American military is, after all, the finest, most efficient, disciplined, and powerful in the world. Externally, it ensures the security of the country. Internally, a universal health care system would ensure the security of each individual's basic health needs.

With the financial collapse of banks and the hand out of trillions of dollars by the U.S. federal government to save American financial institutions, the American people will have to think again about developing an efficient and cost effective system similar to well established and mature systems in other industrialized countries, most of which could be considered socialized medicine.

## Some questions to ask in the search for a solution

Why is it not possible for the richest and most powerful country in the world, with the finest brains and institutions, to devise a universal health care system that is simple and cost effective? Is an ideology more important than the physical security of an individual?

Why shouldn't America learn from some of the best practices of the health care systems of other rich countries, and use that knowledge to create an even better system? Is it national pride that causes this failure to look at systems that are not American? Why not start fresh and create a new system, instead of trying an incremental approach to a fragmented one?

Why is there a lack of vision, when some policy makers and politicians are already aware that the current health care system is unsustainable? Where is the will of these people? What will it take to make them act?

Why not use the latest cutting-edge business practices, such as information technology, to cut down on the cost of health care?

The main question is, is it the basic right of every person in the United States to have health care security, rather than a health care system based on privilege? If so, why not apply a simple, logical, and wise approach to finding appropriate solutions? The answers to all these questions are out there!

The United States of America is ranked number 1 in obesity, 37 in infant mortality rate, and tied at 54 with Fiji for fairness in health care, yet it is spending over 16% of its GDP on health care— the highest per person, by far, in the world! What has gone wrong?

## Action needed

Certain politicians and policy makers need to wake up and not bury their heads in the sand by creating a health care system that is money driven. Incremental changes to the current health care system will only lead to higher costs and less care for the entire population.

Martin Luther King, Jr. stated in one of his speeches, "Of all the forms of inequality, injustice in health care is the most shocking and inhumane." The inequality of health care has steadily increased as more and more people are uninsured and underinsured. The steady rise in bankruptcies—over half of the bankruptcies filed in America are because people are unable to pay their medical bills—is a shocking state of affairs for a rich country like America.

It is time to act. A new health care system must be implemented, one that is inclusive and fair, and provides for each and every person in the nation. Knowledge, facts, and lessons, learned from the experiences of people in America, and in other nations, are out there. Action must be taken on the most important domestic issue of all, creating a universal health care system.

America has the wisest and brightest minds, the finest health care institutions, and more Nobel laureates than the rest of the world. It is not beyond the realm of these people to create a system that is cost effective while covering all of the people in the United States.

Let there be no 'fear factor.' Everyone should be able to visit a doctor and seek treatment, without worrying about money. It is time for politicians and decision makers to leave their ideologies and egos behind, and to implement a universal health care system that provides basic health security for everyone.

As President Roosevelt said, "We have nothing to fear but fear itself." Politicians and decision makers have created the 'fear factor' and other problems associated with the current health system. It is up to the politicians and decision makers to stop the fear-mongering and to resolve the health care issues in order to find superior and cost effective solutions. It is not beyond them. I urge voters to exert pressure on their legislators. I urge Americans to educate themselves.

It is long past time for a call to action. I challenge all politicians and decision makers, and the drug companies, to look beyond profits, and to seek solutions to the American health care crisis together.

## The task ahead

The task of the current administration is to provide a system that is both affordable and accessible, with high-quality performance for all. In making the right choices and decisions on how to solve this issue, they must know all the important facts about the current health care system, and use the wisdom of the many that care about finding a solution to providing universal health security to the people of America.

A commission, carefully chosen by the President and Congress, and with a clear mandate to include all the problems and issues mentioned in chapter 5, should be given time to develop cost effective health care policy suggestions. They should look closely at systems in other rich countries that have been in place much longer than America's while costing 50% less. They should also question such things as why the Singapore health care system has an infant mortality rate of only 2.3 per thousand while in the U.S. it is nearly 6.9. The commission should keep the following points in mind:

- Only a system that combines private and public funds or a publicly funded one that allows top-up insurance would ensure that it did not become money driven, as a privately funded one would do.

- It is important that the system is not a fragmented one, and that it covers the entire population of the country. No health care system in the world has equal accessibility; the important thing is that everyone can access it.

- Adequate money must be spent at all governmental levels to educate people on the importance of disease prevention through diet, exercise, stress reduction, avoiding bad habits, and regular examinations.

- Each state can develop a health care system from the policy suggestions recommended by the commission, for its residents to vote on. The resulting plan can then be implemented by adopting the structure and functions of a Federal Health Board (FHB), as described in chapter 6.

The biggest challenge to reform will be in the following entrenched areas:

- Restricting Lobbyists and their ability to influence politicians

- Replacing fragmented federal and state entitlement programs with one system that serves all segments of society

- Putting decisions about patient care back into the hands of doctors and health care professionals, instead of in the hands of insurance companies

- Reducing the cost of drugs by allowing imports that meet safety standards and regulating expensive and misleading drug advertising

- Reducing the cost of malpractice insurance by bringing frivolous lawsuits under control

The most important new step will be:

- Recognizing the role that information technology and the outsourcing of health services can play in reducing costs

**Closing comment**

The California Universal Health Care bill SB 840, which is essentially a single-payer system, is a good starting point for a universal health care system, even though Governor Schwarzenegger refused to sign it after it passed the state Senate and Assembly in both 2006 and 2008. Basically, it is a publicly funded health care system including all residents of the state.

I believe that President Obama prefers a single-payer universal health care system—a refined form as it is in other rich countries like Norway, Sweden, France, England, and Canada. Obama may get to a single-payer health care system along the lines that President Johnson used to devise Medicare for the elderly.

It is more than likely that the Obama administration will opt for a form of health care system that retains private insurance companies that would compete with some form of government-run health plan similar to existing ones that cover government employees and legislators. In this way, people will voluntarily move out from the private insurance company policies, thus establishing a kind of single-payer universal health care system in two steps.

Another way to achieve universal health care would be in two steps.

The first step is to focus on regulating the existing system to cut costs. Among the cost cutting measures that would have the most effect are:

- The development of extensive, secure IT systems to cut administrative costs

- The development of legislative policies to establish protocols for regulating mal-practice lawsuits in order to eliminate the need for medical professionals to practice defensive medicine

- Requiring insurance companies to insure everybody— including those with existing conditions—and to leave medical decisions in the hand of doctors

- Allowing drug prices to be negotiated with drug companies as is done by the VA

The process of implementing universal care can be aided by a health care reform bill in Congress that would legally trigger insurance companies to reform their practices within 2–5 years or be forced to compete with some form of public option such as a government-run national insurance plan. All of the above could save over $4 trillion over a period of 10 years. The cost of implementing such reorganization, according to many sources, will be about $1 trillion over the same period.

The second step would be to craft a carefully thought out single-payer system with the option of top-up insurance. This could be implemented 5-10 years in the future, saving a further $2 trillion over the following 10 years.

The great American President Thomas Jefferson once said, "Without health, there is no happiness." Let then the administration develop a universal health care system where public views and ideas are given due consideration. I believe that a universal health care system will evolve in the near future that will be accessible, affordable and with a high level of quality of care for every resident in America. And yes, it will be cost effective.

# Epilogue

## Comments on the debate on health care reform in the U. S. Congress, 2009

On one hand, President Obama stated that he would like to implement a single-payer health care system if he could start from scratch. Many Democratic legislators, past and present, including Ted Kennedy, Hillary Clinton, Tom Daschle, John Edwards, Harry Reid, and speaker Nancy Pelosi, agree with him. It is clear that most of the Democratic Party legislators and the Obama administration would like to implement a universal health care reform bill with government sponsored health insurance plans that would compete with those of private insurance companies. Nearly 60% of the American population would like to have a single-payer universal health care system as well, according to a New York Times/CBS News poll in February of 2009. In California, the figure was over 70%.

On the other hand, most Republican legislators and a few Democrats completely dislike the idea of any government run health care plan. They complain that it would eventually turn into a single-payer system because private insurance companies would not be able to compete with a government run system in which health care policy would be dictated by the government. They are against such a system, complaining about the rationing of health care, as they see it, in Europe and Canada, and worrying about who would pay for the initial cost of the reform. They point out that Medicare and Medicaid, already funded and administered by the government, will run out of money in the next ten years.

The single-payer system, used predominantly in the rich countries of Europe, is at least 50% cheaper per person than the current American health care system. Government health care insurance would be run on a non-profit basis and cover everybody, with or without pre-existing conditions. Individuals and small businesses would get to pick between a government sponsored public insurance plan, or a private plan, through a new kind of purchasing pool called an exchange.

Former Senate Majority Leaders of both parties, Daschle, Dole, and Baker, came up with a mish-mash of compromises for a health care reform bill, none of which would cut costs or ensure coverage for everybody in America.

As of August 2009, there were several health care reform proposals in various committees of the House and Senate. In order to have some kind of bi-partisan support for health care reform, Senator Kent Conrad, Chairman of the Senate Budget Committee, called for creation of nonprofit cooperatives to sell insurance in competition with private industry. Senator Baucus, Chairman of the Senate Finance Committee, refused to accommodate any representative from single-payer advocates during hearings in June of 2009 because he is against the idea. Expect the resulting health care reform bill to be neither effective, nor comprehensive, and merely a band-aid.

The six members of the Senate Finance Committee—three Democrats and three Republicans— known as the "Gang of Six," are struggling to get a compromise bipartisan bill to present to Congress while four other legislative committees have passed their health care proposals. The most senior member, U.S. Republican Senator Chuck Grassley from Iowa, made a fear-mongering statement in August 2009, shortly before the death of Senator Ted Kennedy. He suggested that under a British-style, state-run health plan, the Massachusetts democrat would have been denied treatment for cancer because of his age. It was an astonishing statement for Senator Grassley, who is obviously not familiar with the health care systems of other rich countries, to make. Later Grassley told NPR, "I regret using Senator Kennedy's name," but went on to add that he had no regrets about comments he made about British-style health care systems. Comments by Grassley and other American politicians brought severe rebukes from Gordon Brown, Prime Minister of Britain, and David Cameron, Leader of the Conservative Party, both of whom leapt to the defense of the British National Health Service following the vitriolic criticism. Gordon Brown added that the charges were absurd.

Some say that it would cost a $1 trillion over a period of ten years to implement a health care reform plan that would cover most of the population. Senator McCain suggested on C-Span on June 23, 2009, that the cost might be as much as $3 trillion over that period. Senator Baucus has focused his efforts on a deficit-neutral reform bill.

Senator McCain is totally against any government run health care insurance plan, as is Senate Minority Leader Mitch McConnell, as well as most of the Republican senators and House members. McConnell has boasted many times that "We have the best health care system in the world"—he said it again when John King of CNN interviewed him on Sunday, June 14, 2009. McConnell demonizes a government run insurance plan as socialized medicine. He also states that the public does not like decisions about their health care made by the government, and that the government would ration health care.

What seems to be missing in this situation are the following obvious, probing questions that journalists should be asking during interviews with these legislators. If Senator McConnell and others claim, "America has the best health care system in the world," where is the proof, and what are the criteria they are using in making such outrageous statements?

- *Why don't these legislators give up their government sponsored health care insurance plans for themselves and their families, and get health insurance from private companies which offer many choices? Doesn't this make the senators and House members who support neither a single-payer system, nor a government run health insurance plan, hypocrites of the first order?*

- *Why, in what Senator McConnell calls "the best health care system in the world," are nearly 47 million people uninsured and millions more under-insured? If what he says is true, why are more than half the personal bankruptcies in America caused by people who cannot pay their medical bills?*

- *Why, if America has such a great health care system, is the cost of health care commitments to current and retired employees and their families a contributing factor in the bankruptcies of major American car manufacturers and other businesses?*

- *Why do insurance company bureaucrats sitting in a booth somewhere, instead of a doctor, decide which drug or procedure a patient can get? Why does Senator McConnell say that government bureaucrats would make the decisions in a government run plan, when it would actually be doctors?.*

- *Why, in the so-called best health care system in the world, are costs 50% higher per person, than in the next richest country in the world? Why then, does America rank number 1 in obesity, 25 in life expectancy, 27 in infant mortality rate, and number 54 in access to health care, in comparison to other nations? The CIA World Factbook ranks the U.S. life expectancy and the infant mortality rates even higher, at 50 and 44, respectively!*

- *Why is socialized medicine demonized with the fear tactics of rationing and lack of choice? The American Military machine is one of the finest and most efficient in the world. Isn't it funded by taxpayer contributions? Doesn't the government run it? Why isn't the American Military or the VHA referred to as socialized then?*

- *Why don't the senators and legislators who oppose either a single-payer or government-run insurance exchange disclose how much insurance and drug company lobbyists, and other interested parties, contributed to their campaign funds each year for the past five years? Is it the self-interest of these legislators?*

It seems to me that the cost of health care reform is put between one and three trillion dollars over a period of ten years, compared to an American economy of $14 trillion yearly. Many figures regarding the initial cost of health care reform are misleading and some are even false. They do not say how the costs are calculated, or to what kind of universal health care reform package that might emerge from Congress they apply.

The American health care system consumes nearly 30% of revenue in administrative costs and paperwork in a health industry economy of over $2 trillion. These costs are about 10% in other rich countries like France, Japan, and Finland. If there were a reduction of only 33% in these administrative costs, it would save $200 billion per year, which is equal to $2 trillion over a decade. On top of this, if a single-payer health care system were introduced in America, it would save a minimum of another $2 trillion over the same period. This amounts to a combined minimum savings of $4 trillion over ten years, whereas the initial costs involved to switch to a government-run insurance exchange or to a single-payer system are only in the range of $1 trillion, according to various legislative committees. Where is the problem?

A recent article published by CNNMoney.com on August 10, 2009, supports this opinion. It lists the six biggest areas of wasteful spending in American health care. The top two are over testing—which is a large part of defensive medicine—and the inefficient administration and processing of claims. According to PriceWaterhouseCoopers, each of these categories includes over $200 billion a year in wasteful spending. Reducing wasteful expenditures from these two items alone could mean a saving of over $400 billion a year, or $4 trillion over ten years.

Wake up, legislators—stop bickering and posturing! The money for implementing a universal health care system can be found simply through savings made in the current inefficient health care system!

# Reference Notes

## Chapter I

1.  President Jimmy Carter, remarks on Cuban and American health care systems, during his visit to Cuba. (May 2002)

2.  Senator John Kerry, "Health care is a right and not a privilege," speaking at a Democratic Party Unity Dinner (March 25, 2004)

3.  T.R.Reid, former correspondent for the *Washington Post*, *The United States of Europe*, Penguin Press (2005)

## Chapter II

1.  Central Intelligence Agency (CIA), Statistics from the *World Factbook*. (2008)

2.  Organization for Economic Co-operation and Development (OECD) "Health Care Spending as a % of GDP" (includes both public and private spending), (June 2008)

3.  Dr. Michael Marmont and his colleagues, "Americans are much sicker than the English" *The Journal of the American Medical Association (JAMA)* (May 3, 2006)

4.  Harvard Medical School researchers, "Canadians are healthier than Americans,"

5.  *The American Journal of Public Health*, (May 30, 2006)

6.  "Population growth from 1960 to 2002" in selected OECD countries, OECD publication (3rd edition, 2004)

7.　　Statistician Achintya Dey, Center for Disease Control and Prevention (CDC),"Foreign born are healthier than natives" (March 2006)

# Chapter III

1.　　"Australian Government Department of Health and Aging," www.health.gov.au

2.　　"Survey of Australia," the *Economist* (May 7, 2005)

3.　　"Australian Government Health Commission" www.hic.gov.au

4.　　"Health Canada" www.hc-sc.gc.ca

5.　　Health Care Network, "Understanding Canada's Health Care System" (2003)

6.　　Department of Finance, "Investing in Canada's Health Care System" (2003)

7.　　Canadian Institute for Health Information, "National Health expenditure trends," www.cihi.ca (2005)

8.　　"Canada's medical system hit by ruling," the *San Diego Union-Tribune* (June 10, 2005)

9.　　Mike Strobe, "Canadians have better health than Americans," *Associated Press* (May 31, 2006)

10.　　Ministry of Public Health, Cuba, www.cubasolidarity.net

11.　　Jenn Hamm and colleagues, Tulane University, New Orleans, "Health Care in Cuba" www.tulane.edu/~rouxbee/kids98/cuba3.html

12.　　Embassy of France, "The French Health Care System," www.amba.france-us.org/atoz/health.asp

13. Simone Sandier (CREDES) and Marc Durieg, General Directorate of Health, (2004)

14. OECD, "How France Compares," Health at a Glance policy brief, (2005)

15. National Coalition on Health Care, "Health Care in France," (2005)

16. "An Introduction to Healthcare in France," www.frenchentree.com/fe-health

17. CIVITAS, Institute for Study of Civil Society, "French and German Health Care Systems," (2001)

18. "The Price of Popping Pills," the *Economist* (May 15, 2005)

19. Articles on: a) Development of the Healthcare System, b) Healthcare providers, c) Health insurance, d) Remunerations of Healthcare providers, e) Healthcare issues and outlook for the future, www.germanculture.com.ua

20. National Coalition on Healthcare, Washington, DC, "Healthcare in Germany," (2005)

21. "Introduction to the German Healthcare System," www.justlanded.com

22. German Embassy, Washington DC, "Questions and Answers about German Healthcare," www.germany-info.org

23. Department of Health, UK, www.dh.gov.uk/Policyand Guidance

24. Department of Health, UK, "The National Health Service Explained," www.nhs.uk (2004)

25. "NHS in England," www.nhs.uk/england/default.aspx (2005)

26. "Illegal immigrants figure revealed," www.bbc.co.uk

27.    "Britain's Prime Minister still has a chance to leave impressive legacy. But he needs to work fast," the *Economist* (May 7, 2005)

28.    "Health in Britain—Labour messed the National Health Service up at the start, but is now getting it right," the *Economist* (April 23, 2005)

29.    "Healthcare - The Japanese Health Insurance System – Healthcare reforms," www.web-japan/factsheet/health/medical.html

30.    Ministry of Health and Care Services, Labour and Welfare, "Healthcare in Japan," (2005) www.mhlw.go.jp/english/

31.    HealthcareInJapan.hmtl, www.medhunters.com/articles/

32.    Nadeem Esmail, Senior Health Policy Analyst, The Fraser Institute, "Look to Japan on Health," (November, 2004)

33.    "National Health Insurance, Japan," www.jpma.or.jp

34.    Ezra Klein, "Health of Nations, Japan," www.ezraklein.typepad.com/blog/2005/04/health (2005)

35.    National Coalition on Healthcare, Washington, DC, "Healthcare in Japan," (2005)

36.    Ministry of Health and Care Services (Helsdepartementet), Norway, "Healthcare in Norway," (2005), www.odin.dep.no/hod/ministry/org

37.    Paul Van den Noord, Terje Hagen, and Tor Iversen, "The Norwegian Health Care System," OECD report (May 1998)

38.    Ministry of Foreign Affairs (Utenriksdepartementet), Norway, "Norway's Social Security and Health Service," (2005)

39.    Ministry of Health and Care Services, Sweden "Healthcare System in Sweden," www.sweden.se

40.    "Spanish Health Care System," ANCE Publication. www. cne.org

41.    "The Structure of the Health System in Spain," www.sispain. org/english/health/structure.html

42.    Marshall Marinker, Guy's, King's and St. Thomas' Hospitals Medical and Dental School, King's College, London, UK, "The Madrid Framework" (2005)

43.    "Spanish Healthcare" www.spain-info.com/living_in_spain/ spanish-healthcare.htm

44.    "You will require a European Health Card (EHC), you are entitled to free medical and hospital care" (July 1, 2004), www.spain.info

## Chapter IV

1.    Central Intelligence Agency (CIA), "General information and other statistics," *World Factbook* (2005)

2.    Healthcare Timeline from "Health Care Crisis: Who's at Risk?" *PBS* (2000) www.pbs.org/healthcarecrisis/history. htm

3.    The official U.S Government Medicare site (includes Medicare Part A and B, and Medicare Managed Care Plans), www.medicare.gov

4.    United States Department of Health and Human Resources, www.hhs.gov

5.    "Centers for Medicare and Medicaid services," www.cms. hhs.gov/home/medicaid.asp

6.    U.S Department of Veterans Affairs, www.va.gov

7.  Organization for Economic Co-operation and Development (OECD),"Total spending on health per person (public plus private)," www.oecd.org (2003)

8.  Marcia Angell, M.D, Editor-in-chief, expresses her views on Medicare, the *New England Journal of Medicine*

9.  "New Medicare Prescription Drug Benefit," www. whitehouse.gov/news/releases/2005/06/20050616.html

10. Information on Medicare prescription drug coverage, www. medicare.gov/medicarereform/drugbenefit.asp

11. "Prescription Drug Coverage," www.medicare.gov/ pdphome.asp

12. "Medicare Part D – Medicare Supplemental Insurance," www.medicarecaid.com

13. Nairil Chada, Health Care Strategist, "The not so short introduction to health care," www.nairil.com

14. Information on Health Maintenance Organizations (HMOs), www.business.com

15. General information about HMOs along with a list of web sites on the subject, www.calregistry.com/resources/hmo. htm

16. Health Net of California, www.healthnet.com

## Chapter V

1.  Dan Ackman, "Health care costs more, but people buy more," www.forbes.com (June 2005)

2.  "Treasury: Medicare harder to fix than Social Security," www.news.yahoo.com (March 25, 2005)

3.  Vanessa Fuhrman, "Growth in medical costs slows as firm shift tab to workers," the *Wall Street Journal* (November 21, 2005)

4.  Sarah Lueck, "Healthcare spending growth slows," the *Wall Street Journal* (January 10, 2006)

5.  "Desperate measures—America's health care crisis to come" the *Economist* (January 28, 2006)

6.  Dee-Ann Durbin, "GM, UAW reach deal to cut health costs—GM announces plan with UAW to cut health costs, after company loses nearly $3 billion this year," *Associated Press* (October17, 2006)

7.  Sarah Skidmore, "Health care cost for San Diego employees up 61% from 04," the *San Diego Union-Tribune* (November 23, 2005)

8.  "Starbucks: Health insurance costs top its spending for coffee," *Associated Press* (September 15, 2005)

9.  Kris Hudson, "Wal-Mart's low-cost health plan lifts enrollment," the *Wall Street Journal* (December 3-4, 2005)

10. Rafael Gerena-Morales, "U.S needs a new prescription to slow health care spending," the *Wall Street Journal,* (March 6, 2006)

11. Sarah Skidmore, "Golden fears, older Americans are putting off retirement from the workforce to collect benefits and offset increases in health care costs," the *San Diego Union-Tribune (Business section)* (June12, 2005)

12. "Delphi: a helluva a bargaining chip," *Business Week* (October 24, 2005)

13. "Now for the reckoning—corporate America's legacy costs," the *Economist* (October 13, 2005)

14.    Joseph B. White and Jeffrey McCracken, "GM presses UAW for health-care deal," the *Wall Street Journal* (October 14, 2005)

15.    Neal E. Baudette, "Chrysler's salaried employees to pay more for health care," the *Wall Street Journal* (March 16, 2006)

16.    Sarah Karush, "GM shares fall on rise in loss for 2005," the *San Diego Union-Tribune* (March 18, 2006)

17.    Timothy J. Mullaney, "This man wants to heal health care" *Business Week* (October 31, 2005) *Article about Dr. David J. Brailer, who was the top advocate in the Bush Administration for the use of IT in the health care system.

18.    James Kuhnhenn, "Senators Clinton and Gingrich put partisanship on back burner," *Knight Ridder News Service* (2006)

19.    Marc Kaufman, "Poll shows most Americans critical of drug companies," the *Washington Post* (February 25, 2005)

20.    Todd Zoltan, "Drugs and the rising cost of health care," the *San Diego Union-Tribune* Opinion Section (June 30, 2004)

21.    Alex Berenson, "Pfizer to stop advertising pain reliever Celebrex," the *New York Times News Service* (December, 2004)

22.    Theresa Agovino, "Pfizer's uncertain future," *Associated Press* (February, 2005)

23.    Rhonda L. Rundle, "Tenet Hospital faces ban from federal programs," the *Wall Street Journal* (May 9, 2006).

24.    Keith Darcé, "Seniors facing Medicare deadline," the *San Diego Union-Tribune* (May 6, 2006)

25.    Lauren Neergaard, "Pfizer halts Bextra sales at FDA request," *Associated Press medical writer* (April, 2005)

26. Daren Fonda and Barbara Kiviat, "Curbing the drug marketers," *Time Magazine* (July 5, 2005)

27. Robert Langreth and Matthew Harper, "Pushing pills: how the drug industry abandoned science for salesmanship," www.forbes.com (May 8, 2006)

28. Anna Wilde Matthews, "Ghost story: at medical journals, writers paid by industry play big role," the *Wall Street Journal* (December 13, 2005)

29. Dan Vergano, "Study: Medical manuals authors tied to drug-makers," *USA Today* (April 19, 2006)

30. Barbara Mintzes, "Disease mongering in drug promotion: do governments have a regulatory role?" *PLoS Medicine journal (*April 11, 2006)

31. Dana Wilkie, "Lobbying's ills shine through in Medicare law—watchdogs say Congress caved," *Copley News Service* (February 16, 2006)

32. Sarah Skidmore, "The Mexico option: cross-border insurance is a hit with employers and workers," the *San Diego Union-Tribune (Business Section)* (October 16, 2005)

33. Aaron Bernstein and Joseph Weber, "They think they're insured. They're not: Millions of Americans are buying medical 'discount cards' that don't deliver on their promises. Now states are taking action," *Business Week* (December 26, 2005)

34. Robert D. Novak, "A political miscalculation," the *Chicago Sun-Times* (January 9, 2006)

35. Sarah Lueck and Vanessa Fuhrman, "Large insurers are big winners in new Medicare benefit," the *Wall Street Journal* (April 21, 2006)

36. E. J. Mundell, "Medicare Drug Plan gets mixed reviews as deadline arrives," *HealthDay Reporter* (May, 2006)

37.    "Medicare officials hear of pushy drug marketing," *New York Times News Service* (November 27, 2005)

38.    Kevin Freking, "Glitches interrupt Medicare prescriptions," *Associated Press* (January 15, 2006)

39.    Kevin Freking, "Americans to see medical costs rise faster, report finds," the *San Diego Union-Tribune* (February 22, 2006)

40.    Robert J. Samuelson, "It's politics, not the people," *Newsweek* (April 20, 2006)

41.    Joseph Quinlan, "U.S. healthcare in a global context," the *Globalist* (February 2, 2006)

42.    Bill Ainsworth and Cheryl Clark, "Medicare Plan D bleeds state," the *San Diego Union-Tribune* (January 21, 2006)

43.    Staff writer, "No pain, no gain—the drug industry," the *Economist* (August 25, 2005)

44.    Associated Press Business writer, "Workers to bear more healthcare costs," *Associated Press* (September 13, 2005)

45.    "By 2014, feds to pay half of medical costs in U.S.," *Associated Press* (February 24, 2004)

46.    "Report: Cost of drugs growing 60% faster than inflation," *Cox News Service* (September, 2006)

47.    Rhonda L. Rundle, "Tenet to pay $ 725 million to settle Medicare care," the *Wall Street Journal* (June 29, 2006)

48.    Peter Meredith, "The truth about drug companies," interview with Dr. Marcia Angell, www.Motherjones.com (September 7, 2004)

49.    Janet Kornblum, "Crisis in elder care foreseen," *USA Today* (December 12, 2005)

50. "Heading over a cliff on health care," the *Washington Post* (July 2004)

51. "Pfizer reps worldwide—the equivalent of about three U.S army divisions—38,000 people," *Business Week* (February 28, 2005)

52. "Money spent by lobbyists broke record in early 2005; Report cites lack of check on lobbying," the *Washington Post* (2005)

53. Sebastian Mallaby of the Washington Post, "A large public role in health care," the *San Diego Union-Tribune* (January 17, 2006)

54. Vanessa Fuhrmans, "More employers try limited health plans," the *Wall Street Journal* (January 17, 2006)

55. "Sickly no more," the *Economist* (June 10, 2004)

56. Constance Holden MD, "Prescription hazards," Science Now Daily News (2007)

57. Mark Jewell, "Bankruptcy, illness linked—study said to point to health plans' failings," *Associated Press* (February, 2005)

58. "Scalpel, scissors, lawyer—health-care litigation costs America far too much,"
the *Economist* (December 17, 2005)

59. Joseph B. Treaster and Joel Brinkley, "Lawsuits alone can't account for surging malpractice insurance costs," *New York Times News Service* (February 23, 2005)

60. David Brown, "Crisis seen in nation's ER care—capacity, expertise are found lacking," the *Washington Post (June 15, 2006)*

61. Alex Tabarrok, "Price gouging is bad medicine," the *Wall Street Journal* (May 20, 2006)

62. Morton Kondracke, "Medical malpractice suits and errors," the *San Diego Union-Tribune* (February 22, 2005)

63. "Study: Doctors fear of suits hurting care," *Associated Press* (June 2005)

64. Alicia Chang, "40% of malpractice suits called meritless," *Associated Press* (May 11, 2006)

65. Arnold S. Relman, Book review on "The Quality of Health Care Crossing the Quality Chasm: A New Health System for the 21st Century," the *New England Journal of Medicine* (August 30, 2001)

66. David S. Broder, "Health-care meltdown aches for attention," the *Washington Post* (January 6, 2002)

## Chapter VI

1. Morton Kondrake, "Resurrecting the health care debate," the *San Diego Union-Tribune* (*Roll Call*) (June 10, 2005)

2. Steve Leblanc, "Mass. Lawmakers O.K Mandatory Health Bill," *Associated Press* (April 4, 2006)

3. "Massachusetts will require all to have health insurance," *Associated Press* (April 13, 2006)

4. Laura Kurtman, "Schwarzenegger's health plan has critics," *Associated Press* (January 12, 2007)

5. State Senator Sheila Kuehl of California, "Universal Health Care Act SB 840," www.healthcareforall.org/kuehl.html

6. Sara Elizabeth Rogers, "Single payer: California, it's time to have hope," www.healthcareforall.org/kuehl.html (October 19, 2006)

7.     Governor Arnold Schwarzenegger, "I cannot support socialized medicine," the *San Diego Tribune (Opinion)* (September 6, 2006)

8.     Mike Zapler, "State health care bill advances" *San Jose Mercury News*, (December18, 2007)

## Chapter VII

1.     "America's headache: how to start fixing the world's costliest health-care system," the *Economist* (January 28, 2006)

2.     "Asian medical tourism to become multi-million dollar industry," *Yahoo!News* (April 7, 2006)

3.     Jane Zhang, "States take a new look at health reform," the *Wall Street Journal* (May 28, 2006)

4.     Mark Jewell, "Heart device market is hot," *Associated Press,* (December 10, 2005)

5.     Ramola Talwar Badam, "Westerners seek cheap medical care in Asia," *Associated Press* (September 25, 2005)

6.     Robert Samuelson, "The health care system we deserve," *News Week* (January 2006)

7.     Lucy Killea, "UCSD's new vision for health care," the *San Diego Union-Tribune* (April 2005)

8.     Donald L. Barlett and James B. Steele, "Health care can be cured: Here's how," *Time* (Oct. 11, 2004)

9.     Alex Gerber. "Still dragging our feet on universal health insurance," the *San Diego Union-Tribune,* (Opinion) *(*December 30, 2004)

10.     Andres Oppenheimer, "Medical tourism will be next big boom in Latin America," the *Miami Herald* (August 14, 2007)

# Epilogue

11.    Parija B. Kavilanz. "Health care's six money-wasting problems," CNN Money.com,
(August 10, 2009)

# Bibliography

Bookman, Milica Z., and Karla R., *Medical Tourism in Developing Countries*. New York: Palgrave McMillan, 2007

Cohn, Jonathan. *Sick--The Untold Story of America's Health Care Crisis – and the People Who Pay the Price*. New York: Harper Collins, 2007.

Daschle, Tom, with Scott S. Greenberger and Jeanne M. Lambrew. *Critical: What We Can Do About the Health-Care Crisis*. New York: St. Martin's Griffin/Thomas Dunne Books, 2008.

Lamm, Richard D. *The Brave New World of Health Care.* Golden, Colorado: Fulcrum Press, 2004.

LeBow, Dr. Robert H. *Healthcare Meltdown*: *Confronting The Myths and Fixing Our Failing System.* Chambersburg, Pennsylvania: Alan Hood & Co, Inc, 2004.

Maher, Maggie. *Money Driven Medicine*. New York: Harper/ Collins, 2006.

Petersen, Melody. *Our Daily Meds*. New York: Sarah Crichton Books/Farrar, Straus & Giroux, 2008.

Reid, T.R. *United States of Europe*. New York: Penguin Press, 2004.

Relman, Arnold S. *A Second Opinion: How to Prevent the Collapse of America's Health Care.* New York: PublicAffairs, 2007.

Robbins, John. *Diet for a New America*. Tiburon, California: HJ Kramer, 1998.

Robbins, John. *Healthy at 100*. Mississauga: Random House, 2006.

Shultz, George P. and John B. Shoven. *Putting Our House in Order – A Guide to Social Security & Health Care Reform*. New York: W.W. Norton & Co., 2008.

Woodman, Josef. *Patients Beyond Borders*. Chapel Hill, North Carolina: Healthy Travel Media, 2007.

The OECD Health Project: Towards High-Performing Health Systems.
Published by the Organization for Economic Co-operation and Development 2004.

The End

www.ingramcontent.com/pod-product-compliance
Lightning Source LLC
Chambersburg PA
CBHW032059280526
45784CB00012B/175